The Bath Road

History, Fashion, & Frivolity on an Old Highway

Charles G. Harper

Alpha Editions

This edition published in 2021

ISBN : 9789354592911

Design and Setting By
Alpha Editions
www.alphaedis.com
Email - info@alphaedis.com

As per information held with us this book is in Public Domain. This book is a reproduction of an important historical work. Alpha Editions uses the best technology to reproduce historical work in the same manner it was first published to preserve its original nature. Any marks or number seen are left intentionally to preserve its true form.

Preface

This, the fourth volume in a series of books having for its object the preservation of so much of the Story of the Roads as may be interesting to the reading public, has been completed after considerable delay. The DOVER ROAD, which preceded the present work, was published so long ago as the close of 1895, and in that book the BATH ROAD was (prematurely, it should seem, indeed) described as "In the Press." Attention is drawn to the fact, partly in order to point out how quickly and how surely the old-time aspects of the roads are disappearing; for, since the BATH ROAD has been in progress, no fewer than four of the old inns pictured in [Pg x]these pages have disappeared, while great stretches of the road, once rural, have become suburban, and suburban streets have been so altered that they are in no wise distinguishable from those of town. It is because they will preserve the appearance and the memory of buildings that have had their day and are now being swept off the face of the earth, that it is hoped these volumes will find a welcome with those who care to cherish something of the records of a day that is done.

CHARLES G. HARPER.

PETERSHAM,   SURREY,
February, 1899.

I

The great main roads of England have each their especial and unmistakeable character, not only in the nature of the scenery through which they run, but also in their story and in the memories which cling about them. The history of the Brighton Road is an epitome of all that was dashing and dare-devil in the times of the Regency and the reign of George the Fourth; the Portsmouth Road is sea-salty and blood-boltered with horrid tales of smuggling days, almost to the exclusion of every other imaginable characteristic of road history; and the story of the Dover Road is a very microcosm of the nation's history. Nothing strongly characteristic of England, Englishmen, and English customs but what you shall find a hint of it on the Dover Road. As for the Holyhead Road, it traverses the Midland territory of the fox-hunting and port-drinking squires, and reeks of toasts and conjurations of "no heel-taps;" the great North Road is an agricultural route pre-eminently; the Exeter Road the running-ground of some of the fleetest and best-appointed coaches of the Coaching Age; while the Bath Road was at one time the most literary and fashionable of them all.

The best period of the Bath Road was peculiarly the era of powder and patches; of tie-wigs, long-skirted coats, and gorgeous waistcoats; of silk stockings and buckled shoes; when the test of a well-bred gentleman was the making a leg and the nice carriage of a clouded cane; when a grand lady would "protest" that a thing which challenged her admiration was "monstrous fine," and a gallant beau would "stap his vitals" by way of emphasis. It was a period of rigid etiquette and hollow artificiality; but a period also of a grand literary upheaval, and an era in which people were not, as now, merely clothed, but dressed.

Bath at this time was the most fashionable place in all England. Did my lady suffer from that mysterious eighteenth-century complaint "the vapours," she journeyed to "the Bath." Did my lord experience in the gout a foretaste of the torments of that place popularly supposed to be paved with good intentions, he also went to Bath, in his private carriage, cursing as he went; while the halt, the lame, the afflicted of many diseases, came this way; some posting, others by stage-coach, and yet more riding horseback. Every invalid, hypochondriac, and *malade imaginaire* who could afford it went to Bath, for continental spas had not then become possible for English people, and the nauseating waters of Aix, Baden, and other places simply trickled unheeded away.

THE BEGGARS OF BATH

Every invalid, in fact, who could afford it, went to Bath, and the mentally afflicted, who could not go, were sent thither; so that the saying which is now become proverbial (and whose origin and subtle innuendo seem in danger of being lost) arose, "Go to Bath," with the rider, "and get your head shaved;" the lunatics who were sent to those healing waters usually being thus tonsured. This derisive phrase was used toward any one who propounded a more than ordinarily crack-brained project. It is, perhaps, scarcely necessary to say that it has no sort of connection with the modern music-hall vulgarism, "Get your hair cut!"

Another theory—but one more ingenious than acceptable—has it that the phrase derives from Bath having always been a resort of beggars. What, then, more natural, we are asked, than for one accosted by a mendicant to recall this topographical notoriety, and bid the rogue "go to Bath"? For, according to Fuller, that worthy author of the "Worthies," there were "many in that place; some natives there, others repairing thither from all parts of the land; the poor for alms, the pained for ease. Whither should fowl flock in a hard frost but to the barn-door? Here, all the two seasons, being the general confluence of gentry. Indeed, laws are daily made to restrain beggars, and daily broken by the connivance of those who make them; it being impossible, when the hungry belly barks and bowels sound, to keep the tongue silent. And although oil of whip be the proper plaister for the cramp of laziness, yet some pity is due to impotent persons. In a word, seeing there is the Lazar's-bath in this city, I doubt not but many a good Lazarus, the true object of charity, may beg therein." The road, then, to this City of Springs must have witnessed a motley throng.

II

The history of travelling, from the Creation to the present time, may be divided into four periods—those of no coaches, slow coaches, fast coaches, and railways. The "no-coach" period is a lengthy one, stretching, in fact, from the beginning of things, through the ages, down to the days of the Romans, and so on to the era when pack-horses conveyed travellers and goods along the uncertain tracks, which in the Middle Ages were all that remained of the highways built by that masterful race. The "slow-coach" era was preceded by an age when those few people who travelled at all went either on horseback, with their women-folk clinging on behind them, or else were wealthy enough to be able to afford the keep or hire of a "chariot," as the carriages of that time were named. That sinful old reprobate, Samuel Pepys, lived in the last days of the "no-coach" period, and saw the arrival of the slow coaches. He was one of those who used a chariot, and his "Diary" is full of accounts of how, on his innumerable journeys, he lost his way because of the badness of the roads, which then ran through vast stretches of unenclosed, uncultivated, and sparsely inhabited country, and were so fearfully bad that in many places the drivers did not dare to attempt such veritable "sloughs of despond," but drove around them over the hedgeless fields, thus making new tracks for themselves. In this way the origin of the winding character which many of our roads still retain is sufficiently accounted for.

THE "FLYING MACHINE"

The "slow-coach" era was, absurdly enough, that of the "flying machines," and in that era, with the year 1667, the coaching history of the Bath Road may be said to begin, when some greatly daring person issued a bill announcing that a "flying machine" would make the journey. It is not to be supposed that this was some emulator of Icarus or predecessor of the ambitious folks who for the last hundred years, more or less, have been trying to navigate the air with balloons or mechanical flying machines. Not at all. This was simply the figurative language employed to convey to those whom it might concern the wonderful feat that was to be attempted ("God permitting," as the advertiser was careful to add), of travelling by road from the "Bell Savage," on Ludgate Hill, to Bath in three days. But here is the announcement:—

"FLYING MACHINE.

"All those desirous to pass from London to Bath, or any other Place on their Road, let them repair to the 'Bell Savage' on Ludgate Hill in London, and the 'White Lion' at Bath, at both which places they may be received in a Stage Coach every Monday, Wednesday, and Friday, which performs the Whole

Journey in Three Days (if God permit), and sets forth at five o'clock in the morning.

"Passengers to pay One Pound five Shillings each, who are allowed to carry fourteen Pounds Weight—for all above to pay three-halfpence per Pound."

The rush of fashionables to take the waters, and see and be seen, had obviously not then commenced, since one crawling "flying machine" sufficed to accommodate the traffic; and it was not until thirty-six years later that it did begin, when Queen Anne (who, alas! is dead) resorted to "the Bath" for the benefit of the gout. What says Pope?

> "Great Anna, whom Three Realms obey,
> Does sometimes counsel take, and sometimes tay."

If she had taken tea more consistently and drank less port, she would have been just as great and not so gouty—and Bath would have remained in that semi-obscurity in which it had long languished. No crowds of fashionables, no truckling statesmen, no wits, would have hastened down the road and peopled it so brilliantly had not Anne's big toe twinged with the torments of the damned; and it seems likely enough that this book would never have been written. Under the circumstances, therefore, the most appropriate toast for the author and the Mayor and Corporation of Bath to honour is that favourite old one, "High Church, High Farming, and Old Port for Ever," especially the last, "coupling with it," as they used to say before the custom of giving toasts died out, the honoured memory of Queen Anne.

Another three-days-a-week coach then began to ply between London and Bath. In 1711 it had a rival, and five years later saw the establishment of the first daily coach from London. Thomas Baldwin, citizen and cooper of London, saw money in the venture, and, like the hero of one of Bret Harte's verses, who "saw his duty a dead sure thing," he "went for it, there and then." He would seem to have secured it, too, for he held the road for many years against all rivals, and was, moreover, landlord of one of the foremost hostelries on the road—the "Crown," at Salt Hill.

COACHING MISERIES. (*After Rowlandson.*)

His rivals were many, and, considering the popularity to which Bath soon attained, they must all have done well. Indeed, the establishment of a new coach to Bath would now appear to have been a favourite form of speculation, and Londoners found many such advertisements as the following:—

"*Daily Advertiser.* April 9, 1737.
"For Bath.

"A good Coach and able Horses will set out from the 'Black Swan' Inn, in Holborn, on Wednesday or Thursday.

"Enquire of WILLIAM MAUD."

COACHING MISERIES

The invalid who trusted himself to the stage-coach of that period had, however, many risks to run. Doctors might recommend the waters, but before the patient reached them he had to endure a two days' journey, and even at that to bear a very martyrdom of bumps and jolts. For that was just before the time when coach-proprietors began to announce "comfortable" coaches "with springs," just as, a little earlier, they had laid great stress on their conveyances being glazed, and (to skip the centuries) as railway companies nowadays advertise dining and drawing room cars. Here are some coaching woes:—

> "Just as you are going off, with only one other person on your side of the coach, who, you flatter yourself, is the last—seeing the door opened suddenly, and the landlady, coachman, guard, etc., cramming and shoving and buttressing up an overgrown, puffing, greasy human being of the butcher or grazier breed; the whole machine straining and groaning under its cargo from the box to the basket. By dint of incredible efforts and contrivances, the carcase is at length weighed up to the door, where it has next to struggle with various obstacles in the passage."

The pictorial commentary upon this text is appended, together with a view representing passengers refreshed by being overturned into a wayside pond.

The first mail-coach that ever ran in England ran between London and Bristol, and set out on Monday, August 2, 1784. Hitherto the letters had been conveyed by mounted post-boys, often provided with but sorry hacks, and always open to attack at the hands of any bad characters who might think it worth their while to intercept the post-bags. This risk led the more cautious persons, and those whose correspondence was of particular importance, to despatch their letters by the stage-coach, although the cost in that case was 2*s*. as against the ordinary postal charge of only 4*d.* for places between 80 and 120 miles distant.

THE FIRST MAIL COACH

A clever and enterprising man resident at Bath had noted these things. This was John Palmer, the proprietor of the Bath Theatre. He not only noted them, but devised a plan by which the post was rendered swifter and more secure. The stage-coaches of that time took thirty-eight hours to accomplish the journey between London and Bath, and, although safer for the carriage of correspondence than by post-boy, were not so speedy. Palmer had frequently travelled the roads, and he rightly conceived thirty-eight hours to be too long a time to take for a journey of 106 miles. He drew up a scheme for a mail-coach to carry four inside passengers, a coachman, and a guard, and to be drawn by four horses at the rate of between eight and nine miles an hour. In this manner, he argued, the journey between Bath and London should be accomplished, including stoppages, in sixteen hours. This plan, which he made as an instance, to be extended, if successful, to the other main roads throughout the kingdom, he communicated to the General Post Office. Two years passed before Palmer could get his proposals tried, but arrangements were eventually made, agreements entered into with five innkeepers along the London, Bath, and Bristol Road, for the horsing of the coach, and the first mail despatched from Bristol to London, August 2, 1784. The mounted post-boy's day was nearing its close, and by the summer of 1786, the trunk roads knew him and his post-horn no more.

The mail-coaches enjoyed great privileges, of which the greatest was their exemption from all turnpike tolls, and the right exercised by the Post Office of indicting roads which might be out of repair or in any way dangerous. By the year 1810, mail-coaches had increased so greatly that the estimated annual loss of the various turnpike trusts on this exemption was £50,000. And all the while the postal business was increasing by leaps and bounds, although the price of postage was increased from time to time to help supply the Government, which speedily came to recognize the Department as a milch cow, and to demand increasing annual payments from it, to help pay the costs of waging Continental wars.

Let us see what the postage between London, Bath, and Bristol was at different periods. The charges were regulated by distances, and one of the schedule measurements, "exceeding 80 miles and not exceeding 150 miles," just includes these two towns. We find, then, that it was possible to get a letter conveyed that distance in 1635 for 4*d.*, while a bulky package weighing one ounce cost 9*d.* in transmission; not extravagant charges for that far-off time, even allowing for the greater purchasing power of money in the first half of the seventeenth century. Twenty-five years later the scale was altered, and one could despatch a note for a penny less, although it cost 3*d.* more for an ounce weight. From 1711 to 1765, the scale was—

Letter.	One ounce.
4*d.*	1*s.* 4*d.*

and from 1765 to 1784 the charges were again raised, to 5*d.* and 1*s.* 8*d.* respectively. Matters then went from bad to worse. In the beginning of 1797, the figures were 7*d.* and 2*s.* 4*d.*; while the climax was finally reached at the beginning of this century, for on July 9, 1812, it cost 9*d.* to send a note between London, Bath, or Bristol, and 3*s.* for one ounce. A singular fact, in face of these repeated increases, was the growth of the Post Office revenues. In 1796, the net profit was £479,000; ten years later it had risen to considerably over one million sterling. The Bristol profit on Post Office business was £469 in 1794-5, and at that time the postmaster received a salary of £110 per annum. The Bath postmaster's billet was the best in the service, for he received £150, and, moreover, had the assistance of one clerk and three letter-carriers.

PASSENGERS REFRESHED AFTER A LONG DAY'S JOURNEY.
(*After Rowlandson.*)

Meanwhile the stage-coaches had increased greatly. It was about 1800 that the "Sick, Lame, and Lazy"—a sober conveyance so called from the nature of its passengers, invalids, real and imaginary, on their way to Bath—was displaced by the new post coach that performed the journey in a single day; and thus the comfortable, *and* expensive, beds of the "Pelican" at Speenhamland, where "the coach slept," began to be disestablished.

III

"GOD-PERMITS"

Our forefathers of the coaching age were properly pious. Desirous, when they travelled, of a "happy issue out of all their afflictions," as the Prayer-book has it—which in their case included such varied troubles as highwaymen's attacks, being upset, or finding themselves snowed up, with the extreme likelihood in winter-time of being severely frostbitten—they made their wills, and fervently committed themselves to the protection of Providence before starting and putting themselves in the care of the coachman. Coach proprietors, for their part, always advertised their conveyances to run "D.V.;" and the more slangy among our great-grandparents were accordingly accustomed to speak of these coaches as "God-permits." Express trains, which stop for nothing in heaven above or the earth beneath, short of a cataclysm of nature, have relegated that joke to the domains of archæology. Then, however, it had its poignant side.

"The perils of the road in winter and foul weather," says one who braved them, "were formidable. On one occasion I rode sixteen hours under a deluging downpour of rain that never ceased for a single minute, and was so crushing in its effect as to disable every umbrella on the roof before the first hour had elapsed. On another occasion I started at six on a winter's morning outside the Bath "Regulator," which was due in London at eight o'clock at night. I was the only outside passenger. It came on to snow about an hour after we started—a snowstorm that never ceased for three days. The roads were a yard deep in snow before we reached Reading, which was exactly at the time we were due in London. Then with six horses we laboured on, and finally arrived at Fetter Lane at a quarter to three in the morning. Had it not been for the stiff doses of brandied coffee swallowed at every stage, this record would never have been written. As it was, I was so numbed, hands and feet, that I had to be lifted down, or rather, hauled out of an avalanche or hummock of snow, like a bale of goods. The landlady of the 'White Horse' took me in hand, and I was thawed gradually by the kitchen fire, placed between warm pillows, and dosed with a posset of her own compounding. Fortunately, no permanent injury resulted."

SNOWSTORMS

That was as late as 1816. Happily, although the term "an old-fashioned winter," is one frequently employed nowadays to denote one of exceptional severity, there is no reason to believe that such winters were less exceptional then than they are now. But the great frosts and snowstorms of those times belong to history, and although they only occurred (as they do now) at considerable intervals, they bulk largely in the records of the past.

The great snowstorm of December 26, 1836, dislocated the coach service all over the country. The drifts on Marlborough Downs varied in depth from fourteen to sixteen feet. The Duke of Wellington, who was travelling down the road to the Duke of Beaufort's place at Badminton, arrived at Marlborough on the Monday night, in the thick of it, and put up at the "Castle." He was journeying in a carriage and four, with outriders, and started again the next morning, to be promptly stuck fast in a wheatfield. A number of labourers were procured, who dug him out.

On that memorable occasion, the Bath and Bristol mails, which were due at those places on the Tuesday morning, were abandoned eighty miles from London, the mail-bags being brought up by the two guards in a post-chaise with four horses. For seventeen miles they had to come by way of the fields.

Three outside passengers died of the cold when one of the stage coaches reached Chippenham, and frostbites were innumerable.

But if all the untoward coaching incidents were recounted that befell upon the Bath Road, this would resolve itself into a dismal record, and it might then be supposed that coaching was invariably dangerous and uncomfortable, which was not the case. One of the most singular of these happenings was that in which a home-coming sailor was killed. A gunner named John Baker was wrecked on board the frigate *Diomede*, off the coast of Trincomalee, and narrowly escaped being drowned. Being picked up, he recovered sufficiently to be able to take a part in the storming of that place, and was sent home with the ship bearing the despatches. When he set foot again in England, he must naturally have thought all dangers past; but, coming up from Bath in January, 1796, the coach capsized at Reading, and the unhappy gunner, who had survived all perils of battle and the breeze, was killed.

A not dissimilar accident happened in July, 1827, when the Bath mail was overturned between Reading and Newbury, through the horses bolting into a gravel-pit. A naval officer was killed, and most of the passengers injured.

FOGS

Although the latter accident happened in an age of very fast coaches, it is a fact that disasters were actually fewer than they had been in more leisurely times. The reasons for this increased safety in times when speed was vastly greater may be found in the facts that the roads were better kept, and the coaches better built. A whole series of Turnpike Acts had been passed in the course of the previous fifty years, resulting in roads as nearly perfect as roads can be, while the coachbuilder's trade had become almost an exact science.

Had it not been for the occasional recklessness or drunkenness of drivers, and the winter fogs, there would be little to record in the way of accidents. As it was, coachmen sometimes (but very rarely) took a convivial glass too much; or, more often, raced opposition coaches to a final smash; and then there were the "pea-soupers" of fogs, which led the most experienced astray.

The following story belongs to the first quarter of this century, and is told by one of the old drivers: "I recollect," he says, "a singular circumstance occasioned by a fog. There were eight mails that passed through Hounslow. The Bristol, Bath, Gloucester, and Stroud took the right-hand road; the Exeter, Yeovil, Poole, and 'Quicksilver' Devonport (which was the one I was driving) went the straight road towards Staines. We always saluted each other when passing with 'Good night, Bill,' 'Dick,' or 'Harry,' as the case might be. I was once passing a mail, mine being the fastest, and gave my wonted salute. A coachman named Downs was driving the Stroud mail. He instantly recognized my voice, so said, 'Charley, what are you doing on my road?' It was he, however, who had made the mistake; he had taken the Staines instead of the Slough road out of Hounslow. We both pulled up immediately; he had to turn round and go back—a feat attended with some difficulty in such a fog. Had it not been for our usual salute, he would not have discovered his mistake before arriving at Staines."

IV

One of the most striking differences between the coaching age and these railway times lies in the altered relations between passenger and driver. No railway passenger ever thinks of the man who drives the engine. He, in fact, rarely sees him. The coachman, on the other hand, was very much in evidence, and was not only seen, but expected to be "remembered" as well. And "remembered" the old coachmen were, too: for half a crown each to driver and guard was the least one could do in those times. How great a tax this was upon the traveller may be guessed when it is said that the coachman was generally changed about every fifty miles or so. The guard would probably accompany the coach all the way to Bath, but on the longer journeys there were at least two. There was a very simple formula used, as a hint to passengers that a tip should be forthcoming. "I go no further, gentlemen," the coachman would observe, putting his head in at the window. A simultaneous dipping of the hands into fobs on the part of the passengers resulted from this piece of information, and the coachman would depart, richer by considerably over half a sovereign. Imagination does not go to the length of picturing the driver or the guard of a train doing the like.

TIPS

It is not, however, to be supposed that coach passengers greatly delighted in the practice, even in those fine open-handed days. There were many who could not afford it, and others who regarded it as an imposition. But they tipped all the same, because, as Mr. Chaplin, the great coach proprietor in those palmy days, observed, if they did not the guard and coachman "would look very hard at them." Better to face a lioness robbed of her cubs than a coachman defrauded of his tip. Passengers, therefore, resigned themselves with a sigh to the expenditure, and travelled as little as they possibly could. There can, indeed, be no doubt that tipping, grown to a regular system, injured the coach proprietors' business; and it was eventually, if not abolished entirely, at least shorn of its more grandiose proportions. The first man to tackle the question was Thomas Cooper. He was proprietor of a line of coaches running between London and Bristol from 1827 to 1832. "Cooper's Old Company," he called his business. He had originally been landlord of the "Castle Hotel" at Marlborough, but gave it up and removed to Thatcham, where he took a cottage and built stables for his coaching stud. Here he was practically halfway between London and Bristol, and his day and night coaches stopped to dine and sup at "Cooper's Cottage," as, with a sense of the value of alliteration, he called it. All his advertisements bore the announcement, "No fees," and the same pleasing legend was writ large on the backs of his coaches.

Cooper paid his coachmen and guards considerably higher wages, to compensate them for the loss of their tips. He became bankrupt in 1832, and sold his business to Chaplin, who afterwards, through his interest in the railway world, obtained him the post of stationmaster at Richmond, near London. From this position he eventually retired on a pension, and died about fifteen years ago.

We all know the cantankerous passenger in the railway carriage who makes himself objectionable in a variety of ways, but a coach was a much more fruitful source of contention. Fortunately, however, it was not often that the incident of the strong man in the Bath coach bound for London was repeated. A corpulent person of prodigious strength tried to secure a place in the mail, but, all the seats being booked, he was told that it was impossible to convey him that night. Relying upon his strength and the unlikelihood of any one daring to disturb him, he got in while the coach was still standing in the stable yard, and waited. He had to wait so long, and had dined so well, that he fell asleep, and the coachman, finding him there, snoring, put his team into another coach, leaving the fat man in peaceable possession of his seat. He awoke in the middle of the night, still, of course, in the stable yard of the "White Lion" at Bath, while the road echoed with the laughter of the coachman and his friends all the way up to London.

THE "WHITE BEAR," PICCADILLY.

"FULL INSIDE"

In that incident the passengers were fortunate. The "insides" were less to be congratulated who bore a part in the memorable journey down to Bath from Piccadilly with an extra passenger. It is of the Bath mail that the story is told. Mail coaches carried four inside. One night, when the mail was ready to start from Piccadilly, full up, inside and out, a gentleman who wanted to go to Marlborough came hurrying up. He was well known to coachman and guard as a regular customer; but, although they did not want to leave him behind, there seemed to be no alternative. He solved the difficulty himself by squeezing in as the coach started; and so, packed as tightly as herrings in a barrel, they rumbled away, amid the muttered curses of the original occupants. The misery of that journey may be better imagined than described, and when the coach halted at the "Bear" at Maidenhead, it might be supposed that the "insides" would have been only too pleased to get out for a momentary relief when the guard appeared at the door and made what was usually the pleasant announcement, "Time to get a cup of coffee here, gentlemen." Did they get out? Oh no! They were so tightly wedged that they dared not move, afraid lest they should not be able to get in again. So they endured to the bitter end, and there can be no doubt whatever that when Marlborough was reached, they "sped the parting guest" with exceptional heartiness.

SIGN OF THE "WHITE BEAR,"
NOW AT FICKLES HOLE.

The inn from which this coach started was the "White Bear," Piccadilly, which stood, until about the year 1860, on the site now occupied by the Criterion Restaurant. It was a curious old place, chiefly of wood, and had a great effigy of a polar bear on its frontage. This "White Bear" sign is still in existence, but rusticated to the lonely hamlet of Fickles Hole, near Croydon, where it stands in the little garden of the "White Bear" inn.

V

A very swagger stage-coach, the "York House," was started between Bath and London in 1815, followed by a rival, the "Beaufort Hunt." The first-named started from the "York House Hotel" at Bath; the "Beaufort Hunt" from the "White Lion." Both were fast day coaches; and, perhaps because of racing, the "Beaufort Hunt" was upset twice in a fortnight, soon after it had been put on the road. It was a sporting age, but not so sporting that passengers were prepared to risk life and limb in taking part in this keen rivalry. Accordingly, the "Beaufort Hunt" fell upon evil times, and the proprietor had to dismiss his too zealous drivers. He was, however, fortunate in his new coachman, who was exceptionally civil and obliging, and eventually regained the position of the coach, which, although it kept up a furious pace of eleven miles an hour, remained for years a prime favourite with the more dashing travellers along the road.

This and the other crack coaches, which continued running until the Great Western Railway finally took them away on trucks, quite cut out the mails, which, from being the fastest coaches on the road, soon came to occupy a very middling position.

THE AUGUSTAN AGE

In 1821, the mail-coaches had reached a speed of nearly eight and three-quarter miles an hour, including stoppages. They started from the General Post Office at 8 p.m., and reached Bristol at 10 a.m. the following morning. At the same period the two fast stage-coaches just described were doing their eleven miles an hour, and in 1830 were actually timed a mile an hour faster, while the mail was very little accelerated, if at all. Some years later, indeed (in 1837), the Bristol mail was wakened up, and performed the 121 miles in 11 hrs. 45 min., or at the rate of ten miles and a quarter an hour, including changes, of which there were fourteen. This was the fine flower of the Coaching Age on the Bath Road. There were then about fifteen or sixteen day and night coaches between London and Bath, and two mails, all running full. On June 4, 1838, the Great Western Railway was opened as far as Slough, and the coaches ran only between that place and Bath. In March, 1840, the railway was open as far as Reading; and June 30, 1841, saw trains running between London, Bath, and Bristol, and the road deserted.

The difference between those times and these is sufficiently striking to demand some attention. Fares by mail were 4*d.* a mile; by stage-coach, from 4*d.* to 3½*d.* a mile inside, and 2*d.* outside. Or, if one wanted to travel somewhat cheaper, and did not mind an all-night journey, the fares by night coach were about 2½*d.* and 1½*d.* respectively. The cost of travelling to Bath was therefore anything from 35*s.* down to 14*s.* To these figures 5*s.* or 6*s.* should be added, for coachmen and guards always expected to be tipped, while something like half a sovereign for refreshments was essential.

For those whose time was of no consequence, and whose pockets were not well lined, there were the slow lumbering stage-waggons, which progressed at about four miles an hour and stopped everywhere. The fare by these was something under a penny a mile, and refreshments were correspondingly cheap, for the landlords of the wayside inns, who despised this kind of travellers, provided a supper of cold beef at 6*d.* a head, and a shake-down of clean straw in the stable-loft at a nominal price.

If, on the other hand, one desired to do the thing in style, it was always possible to post down. Only the great men of the earth did that, for the cost was more than considerable, tolls alone for a carriage and pair amounting to 9*s.* In fact, posting pair-horse to Bath would not have cost less than £11. Nor would there then have been any advantage in pace, for post-chaises generally attained a speed of ten miles an hour, when the best coaches were doing twelve. Still, there were those who posted, ready to pay, both in money and time, for their privacy; for the wealthy Briton of that day was apt to be an extremely haughty and insufferable person, and preferred to travel like a Grand Llama, even though he paid heavily for it in coin and discomfort.

THE FIRST MOTOR-CAR

Almost the last scene in this "strange eventful history" of road-travelling in the past was enacted in 1829, when Mr. Gurney's "steam-carriage" conveyed a number of people from London to Bath. The vehicle did not meet with the approval of the rustics, and at Melksham an angry mob, armed with stones, assailed the travellers, loudly denouncing the unholy thing. From Cranford Bridge to Reading, the speed was at the rate of sixteen miles an hour, and so delighted were those concerned with the result of the experiment that an announcement was made that "immediate measures" would be taken "to bring carriages of the sort into action on the roads." It has, however, been left to these last few years to re-introduce the motor-car, with results yet to be seen.

Such was travel on the road in olden times. To-day one travels to Bath in a fraction of the time at less than half the cost; the 107 miles railway journey from Paddington occupies exactly two hours, and a third-class ticket costs 8*s.* 11*d.*

As these lines are being written, the last of the old coaching inns from which some of the Bath stages started, is being demolished. The "White Horse," in Fetter Lane, Holborn, fell upon evil days when railways revolutionized its custom. Where Lord Eldon stayed in 1766, and whence many another aristocratic traveller set forth, tramps and fourpenny "dossers" found refuge. The "White Horse" inn became the "White Horse Chambers"—not the kind of chambers understood in St. James's, but rather the cheap cubicles of St. Giles's.

THE "WHITE HORSE" INN, FETTER LANE. DEMOLISHED 1898.

DEPARTED GLORIES

Cary's "Itinerary" for 1821 (Cary was a guide, philosopher, and friend without whom our grandfathers never travelled) gives no fewer than thirty-seven stage-coaches which started from this old house. There was the "Accommodation" to Oxford, at seven o'clock in the morning; the Bath and Bristol Light Post coach, at two in the afternoon, arriving at Bristol at eight o'clock the following morning; and the Worcester, Cheltenham, and Woodstock coaches, which all travelled along the Bath road to Maidenhead. Then there were the York "Highflier," a crack Light Post coach, every morning, at nine o'clock; the "Princess Charlotte," to Brighton; the Lynn, Dover, Cambridge, Ipswich, and other coaches too numerous to mention in detail. It will, therefore, not be surprising to learn that the stables of this busy hostelry were large enough to hold seventy horses.

At the foot of the staircase, near the entrance, was the office, and everywhere were long passages and interminable suites of rooms. But how different the circumstances in later years! The vast apartment that was the public dining-room became, in fact, a kind of socialistic kitchen.

There, when his day's work was done, the kerbstone merchant came to grill the cheap chop he had purchased. There the professional cadger toasted a herring, while his companions cooked scraps of meat or toasted cheese.

This part of Holborn was once famous for its old inns. Indeed, on the opposite side of that main artery of traffic were the "Black Bull" and the "Old Bell." There is nothing left of the first now except the great black effigy of a bull with a golden zone about the middle of him, and beyond the archway a courtyard which was once the galleried courtyard of the inn, but is now just the area of a block of peculiarly dirty "model" dwellings.

COURTYARD OF THE "OLD BELL," HOLBORN. DEMOLISHED 1897.

THE "OLD BELL"

What Londoner did not know the "Old Bell" Tavern, in Holborn, whose mellowed red brick frontage gave so great an air of distinction to that now commonplace thoroughfare. Among the last of the old galleried inns, some of its timbers dated back to 1521. The front of the house was comparatively juvenile, dating only from 1720. What its galleried courtyard was like let this sketch record. The site was sold for £11,600, and the house demolished, at the close of 1897, although its structural stability was unquestioned, and the place a favourite dining and luncheon house. Twenty-one coaches left that old house daily in the full flush of the coaching age; among them two Cheltenham coaches, the coaches to Faringdon, and Abingdon, Oxford, Woodstock, and Blenheim, all of which went by the Bath Road so far as Maidenhead, where they branched off *viâ* Henley. In addition, there was the stage which ran twice a day to Englefield Green, branching off at Hounslow. The "Old Bell" could, indeed, claim the credit of being the last actual coaching-house in London, for it is only a few years since the last three-horsed omnibus was discontinued that ran between it and Amersham, in Bucks. When the Metropolitan Railway extension reached that place, the conveyance, of course, became quite unnecessary, and the last remote echo of the genuine coaching age died away.

VI

The Bath Road is measured from Hyde Park Corner, and is a hundred and five miles and six furlongs in length. The reasons for this being reckoned as the starting-point of this great highway are found in the fact that when coaches were in their prime, Hyde Park Corner was at the very western verge of London. Early in the eighteenth century Londoners would have considered it in the country; and, indeed, the turnpike gate which until 1721 crossed Piccadilly, opposite Berkeley Street, gave a quasi-official confirmation of that view. In that year, however, it was removed to Hyde Park Corner, just westward of the thoroughfare now known as Grosvenor Place, and so remained until October, 1825, when it was disestablished in favour of a turnpike gate opposite the spot where the Alexandra Hotel now stands. Beyond it—in the country—was the pretty rural village of Knightsbridge, with a gate by the barracks; and, beyond that, the remote village of Kensington, to which the Court retired for change of air, far away from London and its cares!

From 1721 to 1825, therefore, we may well regard Hyde Park Corner as the beginning of town. This was so well recognized that local allusions to the fact were plentiful. For instance, where Piccadilly Terrace now stands was an inn called the "Hercules' Pillars," a favourite sign for houses on the outskirts of large towns, just as churches dedicated to St. Giles were anciently placed outside the city walls. "Hercules' Pillars" was the classic name for the Straits of Gibraltar, regarded then as the boundary of civilization; hence the peculiar fitness of the sign.

On the western side of this inn, a place greatly resorted to by the 'prentice lads who wanted to take their lasses for a country outing in Hyde Park, was a little cottage, long known as "Allen's Stall," which stood here from the time of George the Second until 1784, when Apsley House was erected on its site. The ground is said to have been a present from George the Second to a discharged soldier named Allen, who had fought under his command at Dettingen.

ALLEN'S STALL AT HYDE PARK CORNER, ABOUT 1756.

ALLEN'S STALL

The story is a pretty one, and tells how the King was riding into Hyde Park, when he noticed the soldier, still wearing a tattered uniform, taking charge of the stall in company with his wife.

"What can I do for you?" asked the King, replying to the military salute which the ragged veteran offered.

HYDE PARK CORNER, 1786.

"I ask nothing better than to earn an honest living, your Majesty," replied the soldier; "but I am like to be turned away by the Ranger. If your Majesty were to give me a grant of the ground my stall stands on, I would be happy."

"Be happy, then," answered the King, and saw to it that Allen had his request satisfied.

The stall became a cottage, where Allen and his wife lived until they were gathered to the great majority, having in the meanwhile, it may be supposed, done pretty well for themselves, since we find their son to have been an attorney. The cottage was deserted, and the royal gift of the land partly forgotten, so that the Lord Chancellor of that period was granted a lease of the ground and began to build a mansion on it. Allen's son had to the full that shrewdness which has made the name of "attorney" so generally detested that those "gentlemen by Act of Parliament" prefer nowadays to call themselves "solicitors." He waited until my Lord Chancellor had nearly completed his house, and then put forward his claim, finally obtaining £450 per annum as ground rent. He subsequently sold the land outright, and so Lord Chancellor Henry Bathurst, Baron Apsley, and Earl Bathurst, became the freeholder, and named his residence "Apsley House." The mansion was purchased by the nation for the great Duke of Wellington in 1820. It was, from its situation, long known as "No. 1, London."

VII

MUD BULWARKS

Let us see what kind of entrance to London this was in olden times. In Queen Mary's day the idea of a road leading so far as Bath seems to have been considered too fantastic for common use, and this was accordingly known as the "waye to Reading." In that reign, which was so reactionary that many were discontented with it, and roused up armed rebellions, the rebel Sir Thomas Wyatt brought his men thus far, having crossed the Thames at Kingston and struggled through the awful sloughs between that place and Knightsbridge. It seems quite likely that, but for the mud of those miscalled "roads," the rebellion would have been successful, and the course of history changed. But Wyatt's soldiers were utterly exhausted with the march; and when the Londoners saw them, plastered with mud from head to foot, they forgot their own discontent, and laughed at their would-be deliverers, calling them "draggle-tails." So, dispirited and contemned, they were easily disposed of by the Queen's troops, who, secure behind their girdle of muck, had only to wait and slay them at leisure.

HYDE PARK CORNER, 1792.

The lesson seems not to have been lost upon the authorities, and accordingly we find this defence of dirt in existence up to the year 1842. For nearly three hundred years this "splendid isolation" set an almost impassable gulf between those who wished to get out of London and those who wanted to come in; for in the year just mentioned we learn that Knightsbridge was in so deplorable a state of neglect that it was perfectly impassable for persons possessing a common regard for cleanliness or comfort. Ankle-deep in mud and water, the pavement was rendered additionally dangerous by two steps, forming a sudden descent, so that those who were rash enough to attempt to pass that way in the dark generally bruised themselves severely at the best of it; or, at the worst, broke a leg or an arm.

But this was nothing compared with a former age, when Lord Hervey, writing from Kensington, said the road was so infamously bad that he lived there in a solitude like that of a sailor cast away upon a lonely rock in mid-ocean. The only people who enjoyed this condition of affairs appear to have been the footpads and the highwaymen, who had the very best of times, until they were caught. Indeed, in the days when the stage-coaches performed the then marvellous feats of travelling at anything from three to five miles an hour, under favourable circumstances, the road could not be considered safe after Hyde Park Corner was left behind; and records tell of highway robberies, with the romantic accessories of blunderbusses and horse-pistols, at Knightsbridge so late as 1799.

HYDE PARK CORNER, 1797.

THE "HALFWAY HOUSE"

There was at that time, and until 1848, an old inn standing by the way, near where are now Knightsbridge Barracks. This inn, the "Halfway House," occupied the exact site where Prince of Wales's Gate now gives access to Hyde Park. Hereabouts lurked all manner of bad characters, who had infested the neighbourhood from time immemorial, safe from the clutches of the law both in their numbers and in the isolation created by the almost bottomless sloughs of mud which then decorated what was, by courtesy or force of habit, called the "road."

THE "HALFWAY HOUSE." 1848.

At this spot, in April, 1740, the Bristol mail was robbed by a footpad, who overpowered the post-boy and got off with both the Bath and Bristol bags; while in 1774, three men were hanged for highway robbery here. But the most thrilling and circumstantial story of highwaymen at this spot is that which relates the capture of William Belchier, in 1750. There had been numerous highway robberies in the neighbourhood of the "Halfway House," and at last one William Norton, a "thief-catcher," was sent to apprehend the man, if possible. He took the Devizes chaise at half-past one in the morning of June 3, and when they had come to the place, sure enough the robber was there, waiting for them, and on foot. He bade the driver stop, and, holding a pistol in at the window, demanded the passengers' money. "Don't frighten us," replied Norton. "I have but a trifle; you shall have it." He also advised the three other passengers to give up their coin; and, holding a pistol concealed in one hand and some silver in the other, let the robber take the money. When he had taken it the thief-taker raised his pistol and pulled the trigger. It missed fire; but the robber was too frightened to notice that. He staggered back, holding up both hands, exclaiming, "O Lord, O Lord!" Norton then jumped out after him, pursued him six or seven hundred yards, and then caught him. He begged for mercy on his knees, but Norton took his neck-cloth off, tied his hands, and brought him into London, where he was tried, found guilty, and hanged. The prisoner asked his captor in court what trade he followed. "I keep a shop in Wych Street," replied Norton; adding, with grim significance, "and sometimes I take a thief."

In Kensington Gore (which might have obtained its sanguinary name from these encounters—but didn't) a certain Mr. Jackson, of the Court of Requests at Westminster, was requested to "stand and deliver" on the night of December 27, in the same year, by four desperadoes. And so the tale goes on, with such curious side-lights on the state of society as are afforded by the stories of how pedestrians, desirous of journeying from London to Knightsbridge and Kensington, were used in those "good old times" to wait in Piccadilly until there were gathered a sufficient number of them to render the perilous journey safer. Even then they did not rely only on their numbers, but went well armed with swords, pistols, and cudgels.

TURNPIKE GATES

It is scarcely to be supposed that the turnpike-gates earned much money in those times, when ways were foul and dangerous, and when the cut-throats who lurked about that delectable "Halfway House" were in their prime. Printed here will be found several views of the first gate, showing its development from 1786 to 1797. It will be seen that a high brick wall then bounded the Park. This was continued all the way, except where the houses, low inns, and cottages on the north side of the road stood, and where their successors stand to-day, to the eastward and westward of the present "Albert Gate." That imposing entrance to the Park was made in 1846, and the immense houses on either side—the "two Gibraltars," as they were called—built. They were so called because it was thought they would never be taken; but the one on the east side, now the French Embassy, was soon let to Hudson, the Railway King. As mentioned just now, the "Halfway House" stood where the Prince of Wales's Gate opens into the Park. It stood there until 1848, when the ground was purchased for £3000, and the house pulled down. If the owners had kept the land, their descendants to-day could have sold it for a sum that would represent a handsome fortune, as evidenced by the fact that a plot of ground of the same size, on which Thorney House stood, in Kensington Gore was sold in 1898 for £100,000. Thus does the value of land increase in the neighbourhood of London.

In 1827, London and its neighbourhood began to be relieved of the incubus of the turnpike-gates. In that year twenty-seven toll-gates were removed by Parliament; eighty-one were disestablished July 1, 1864; and sixty-one, October 31, 1865. Many others were swept away on the Essex and Middlesex roads on October 31, 1866, while the remainder ceased July 1, 1872. The first toll-gate which gave the traveller pause from 1856 to July 1, 1864, on the Bath and Exeter roads stood in Kensington Gore, and barred the roadway just where Victoria Road branches off. Many yet living can recall the "Halfpenny Hatch," as it was familiarly known. At the time of the Great Exhibition of 1851 the road was distinctly rural. It was that greatest of all exhibitions which gave an impetus to building in this neighbourhood. Up to that time London had not "discovered" Kensington, and the highway was not a mere street, but looked as though the country were round the corner, which, indeed, was very nearly the case. You could then, in fact, well imagine yourself to be on the highway to somewhere or another—a thing demanding more imagination to-day than most people are capable of calling up.

VIII

KENSINGTON HIGH STREET, SUMMER SUNSET.

OLD KENSINGTON

It may be as well to put on record in this place the Kensington of my own recollection. My reminiscences of Kensington by no means go so far back as the time when Leigh Hunt wrote his "Old Court Suburb," a book which described what was then a village "near London;" but when I first knew that now bustling place it was, if not exactly to be described as rural, certainly by no stretch of imagination to be called urban. In those days the great shops, which are no longer called shops, but "emporia," or "stores," or "magazines," did not flaunt with plate-glass windows opposite St. Mary Abbot's Church, nor, indeed, did the present building of St. Mary exist. In its place was a hideous structure, erected probably at some early period of the eighteenth century. It had windows that purported to be Gothic, and a bell-turret that belonged to no known order of architecture. It, and the now demolished old church of St. Paul, Hammersmith, bore a singular likeness to one another. The present generation can only discover what these unlovely buildings were like by referring to old prints, because there are none other now existing in London to which they can be likened; and a very good thing too. I can recollect old St. Mary's very well indeed, and the days when the old Vestry Hall was still a place for the transaction of vestry business are quite vivid to me. In fact, at that time the Vestry Hall was somewhat new, and where the imposing Town Hall now stands beside it there was a tall building of very grimy brick, with quaint little figures of a boy and a girl perched high up on brackets above, and on either side of, the door. These little figures were represented as clad in a peculiar Dutch-like uniform; the boy, I think, blue, and the girl a quite painful orange, whenever they repainted her, which was seldom. This was, in fact, some sort of charity school, and it was as dismal a place as all charitable institutions were apt to be in our grandfathers' time, when it was criminal to be poor, and eleemosynary establishments, in consequence, were designed as much like prisons as might well be.

"OLDEST INHABITANT."

At the time of which I speak it was quite necessary to go to London to do any save the most ordinary shopping, and if one had told the "oldest inhabitant" that a time was presently coming when it would be possible not only to order, but to purchase and take away on the instant, from Kensington shops the rarest and most costly things that the heart of man (or woman either, for that matter) could desire, that ancient individual would have thought he was being told fairy tales.

I knew that oldest inhabitant, who has been long since gathered to his fathers. His was a quaint figure, and he was stored with many reminiscences. He could "mind the time" when Gore House was occupied by the Countess of Blessington, and when Louis Napoleon, then a young man about town, was a frequent visitor to that somewhat Bohemian establishment. Also he remembered the first 'bus to make its appearance in Kensington. For myself, I certainly remember the time here when omnibuses were few and far between. Now there are generally half a dozen waiting at any time you like to mention by St. Mary Abbot's, which has become, in omnibus slang, "Kensington Church," while the pavements are thronged by fashionable crowds all day long and every day. Not least remarkable is the long row of bicycles drawn up against the kerb opposite the aforesaid emporia, in charge of a diminutive boy in buttons, the patrons of these great shops being inveterate "bikists."

THE NEW KENSINGTONS

Now that towering hotels and flats have been built in Kensington High Street, the old-time distinction of the "Old Court Suburb" is fast becoming obliterated, and there are more Kensingtons than were ever dreamed of years ago. North Kensington, and South and West Kensington—which, shorn of these would-be aristocratic aliases, are just Notting Hill, Brompton, and Hammersmith—were just so many orchards and market-gardens not so many years ago; and I declare that it is not so long since there was an orchard in Allen Street, off the High Street, where red-brick flats now stand, while, in that chosen realm of flatland, Earl's Court, the cabbages and lettuces grew amazingly. Cromwell Road was not built at the time to which my memory harks back, and where the ornate Natural History Museum now stands there was a huge gravel-pit, in which were many ponds and swamps, where wild grasses grew and slimy newts increased and multiplied greatly. Gore House, which had been Lady Blessington's, was still standing in the early years of my recollection, and the Albert Hall, which now occupies the site of it, was, consequently, undreamt of. The last use to which it had been put was to be converted, by Alexis Soyer, into a huge restaurant for the millions who frequented the Great Exhibition of 1851, which I do *not* recollect, thank goodness!

KENSINGTON HOUSE

There were other landmarks in the Kensington of my youth which have long since been swept away. For instance, where Victoria Road joins the Gore there was a tall archway leading to a hippodrome, or horse repository. Where it stood there is now an extremely "elegant"—as they used to say when I was younger—hotel. Even greater changes have taken place where the Gore joins the High Street. Where that collection of palatial houses called Kensington Court now stands, there stood years ago a huge old brick mansion which in its last days experienced some strange vicissitudes of fortune, among which its last two changes—into a school for young ladies, and finally into a lunatic asylum—were not the least remarkable. There was in those days a most dreadful slum at the back of this mansion, known locally as the "Rookery." Londoners should know the history of Kensington Court and its site, and how Baron Albert Grant, in the heyday of his financial success, pulled down the old mansion, and built himself on its ruins a lordly (and vulgar) pleasure-palace, which he called "Kensington House." The memory of it springs fresh to this day, and it requires little effort to recall the place as it stood, in all its pristine pretentiousness, until 1880, or thereabouts. It was built by the redoubtable Baron to shame Kensington Palace, which it exactly faced, and if gilt railings, fresh white stone, and big plate-glass windows may be said to have put the old Palace out of countenance, then Kensington Palace was shamed indeed, but only with that very questionable kind of shame which overtakes the poor patrician confronted by a swaggering, pursy millionaire. At any rate, Kensington Palace is avenged, for not one stone now remains of that pretentious house. It lay back some little distance from the road, from which it was screened by a tall iron railing, with gilded spikes and globular gas-lamps at intervals, of a type closely resembling those in use on the Metropolitan and District Railways. It is not a lovely type, but it is one still greatly favoured in the suburbs of Clapham and Blackheath.

This ornate palisade of cast-iron, which pretended to be wrought, once passed, a gravel drive led up to the house. Ah, that house! It possessed all the flamboyant glories of Grosvenor Gardens and more, and was of a style called variously by the building journals of that day, French or Italian Renaissance. "Renaissance" is a term which, like charity, covers a multitude of sins, and if you want to cloak a collection of architectural enormities, why, you term it Renaissance, and, by implication, insult the great French and Italian masters of the New Birth. It needs not to trouble about the details of that house, save to say that polished granite pillars were well to the fore, and that portentous Mansard roofs in fish-scale lead coverings, with spikes, finished off its sky-line. For long years Kensington House remained unlet, because of the immense sums its up-keep would have entailed. Millionaires, South African and other varieties, were not so plentiful years ago as they are now. So, after some years of forlorn waiting for the occupier who never came, Kensington House, never once inhabited, was at last demolished, and its materials sold. It is said that the grand marble staircase went to grace the gilded salons of Madame Tussaud's waxen court, and certainly the spiky railings, with their gas-lamps, were sold to furnish an imposing entrance to Sandown Park Racecourse, where they may be seen to this day by the cyclist who wheels through Esher, down the Portsmouth Road.

THACKERAY'S HOUSE, YOUNG STREET.

JOHN LEECH

THE "WHITE HORSE."
TRADITIONAL RETREAT
OF ADDISON.

There still stands, off High Street, the grimy double-bayed house, now numbered 16, Young Street, but formerly No. 13, in which Thackeray wrote "Vanity Fair;" but most others of the old literary and artistic haunts of the "Old Court Suburb" have been demolished. "The Terrace"—that long row of old-fashioned houses extending from Wright's Lane westward—was pulled down but six years ago. Those houses were not beautiful, but they were at least pleasingly old-fashioned, and in No. 6 lived and died John Leech, an early victim of that peculiarly modern malady, "nerves." Some amazingly up-to-date shops now occupy the spot.

Long ago, the other old-fashioned houses on this side of the road lost their forecourt gardens, over which other shops were built; and beyond the memory of any one now living there stood a little country inn at the corner of what is now the Earl's Court Road; a rural retreat called the "White Horse," to which Addison withdrew from the cold splendours of Holland House opposite. He had contracted an unhappy marriage with the Countess of Warwick, the mistress of that splendid mansion, which happily yet remains; but stole away to this more congenial haunt, and drank his intellect away.

Beyond this, all was country road, in the coaching days, until Hammersmith was reached. The first outpost of that now unsavoury place was a rural inn called the "Red Cow," opposite Brook Green.

IX

THE "RED COW"

The "Red Cow," pulled down December, 1897, rejoiced once upon a time in the reputation of being a house of call for the peculiar gentry who infested the suburban reaches of the great western highways out of London. It was not by any means the resort of the aristocracy of the profession of highway robbery; but a place where the cly-fakers, the footpads, and the lower strata of thievery foregathered to learn the movements of travellers and retail them to the fine gentlemen who, mounted on the best of horses, and clad in gorgeous raiment, occupied the higher walks of the art at a safer distance down the road. The house was built in the sixteenth century, and was a quaint, though unpretending roadside tavern with a high-pitched, red-tiled roof. It possessed vast stables, for it was situated, in early coaching days, at the end of the first stage out of London. It may well be imagined, then, that the stable-yard was a scene of constant excitement in the good old days, for here were kept a goodly supply of strong roadsters for the coaches running to Bath, Bristol, Wells, Bridgewater, and Exeter, and here the elegant samples of horseflesh which had brought the coaches at a spanking pace from the "Belle Sauvage," on Ludgate Hill, were changed for animals who could do the rough work of the country roads. They were not particularly fine to look at—especially those used on the night coaches—and it was often a matter of surprise that they were able to keep up the pace required, and that the greasy old harness stood the strain. It has been said that in one of the old-fashioned rooms of the "Red Cow" E. L. Blanchard wrote his "Memoirs of a Malacca Cane." In the last thirty years or so of its existence the "Red Cow" was a favourite pull-up for the waggoners from the market gardens, who in the small hours of the morning rumbled past with piled-up loads of fruit, vegetables, and flowers for Covent Garden, and halted on their return for a refresher of bread and cheese and beer. Then, too, the hay-carts used to halt here, and the sight of them, with the horses drinking from the old wooden water-trough beside the kerb-stone, underneath the swinging sign, was like a picture of Morland's come to life, and agreeably leavened that general air of fried-fish, drink, and dissipation which lingers in the memory as the most characteristic features of modern Hammersmith.

THE "RED COW," HAMMERSMITH. DEMOLISHED 1897.

The travellers who were whirled through this place in the Augustan age of coaching were soon in the country again, on the way to Turnham Green, along the Chiswick High Road. That fine broad thoroughfare is now bordered by an almost continuous row of modern shops, erected, many of them, where barns and ricks stood less than ten years ago. Such was the appearance of "Young's Corner," indeed, until quite recently. That corner, let it be said for the information of those not well acquainted with the topography of the western suburbs, is the spot where the road from Shepherd's Bush joins the highway. Let it further be placed on record, before "historic doubts" have had time to gather about the origin of the name, that it derives from a little grocer's shop kept at the north-east angle of that junction of the roads within the recollection of the present writer, by one Young, who has probably been long since gathered to his fathers, for his Corner knows him no more, and a house-agent's shop, a brand-new building (like all its neighbours), stands where the now historic Young sold tea and sugar, and (let us hope) waxed prosperous in days gone by.

TURNHAM GREEN

Turnham Green lies ahead: a place historic by reason of a preliminary skirmish in the Civil War between Cavaliers and Roundheads, and the residence in the early part of the century of a peculiarly heartless murderer. The passengers by the two-horsed "short-stages" which in the first half of this century travelled from London to the outlying villages and halted at the "Pack Horse and Talbot," doubtless were curious regarding Linden House, near by, notorious from association with Thomas Griffiths Wainewright, author and poisoner. He was born at Chiswick in 1794, and was a grandson of Dr. Ralph Griffiths of Turnham Green. He began life by serving in the army, but presently took to literature as a profession, and wrote voluminously in the magazines of that day. As an author, although possessed of a sprightly wit, he would long since have been forgotten had it not been for the sensational career of crime upon which he entered in 1824. In that year he forged the signatures of his trustees, in order to obtain possession of a sum of £2259. He induced his uncle, Mr. G. E. Griffiths, of Linden House, to receive him there as an inmate. Within a few months his relative died, poisoned with nux vomica, and Wainewright came into possession of his property. In 1830 he persuaded a Mrs. Abercromby, a widow lady, to take up her abode with him and his wife at Linden House. She came with her two daughters and was promptly poisoned with strychnine. After this he removed from the neighbourhood, and embarked upon a further series of murders in London. Eventually detected, he was convicted and transported for life to the Australian colonies, where he is credibly said to have poisoned others. Murder by poison was, in fact, an obsession with this man, although he was sufficiently sane and sordid to select victims whose deaths would bring him pecuniary advantage. Wainewright's *métier* in literature was chiefly art criticism, and his style narrowly resembles that of a revolting person, now ostracised from Society, who also dabbled in Art and actually wrote and published an "appreciation" of the poisoner some few years since.

Linden House was pulled down some fifteen years ago, and its site is marked by the modern villas of Linden Gardens. The recollection of it brings a train of reminiscences.

X

SUBURBAN CHANGES

Reminiscences are soon accumulated in these times. It needs not for the Londoner to be in the sere and yellow leaf for him to have known many and sweeping changes in the pleasant suburbs which used to bring the country to his doors, and the scent of the hawthorn through his open window with every recurring spring. For myself, I am not a lean and slippered pantaloon, on whose head the snows of many winters have fallen. The crow's-feet have not yet gathered around the corners of my eyes; and yet I have known many rural, or semi-rural, villages around the ever-spreading circle of the Great City which in my time have been for ever engulfed in the on-rolling waves of bricks and mortar. It is no effort of memory for me, or for many another, to recall the market gardens, the orchards, the open meadows, and the fine old seventeenth and eighteenth century red-brick mansions, each one enclosed within its high garden walls, with the jealous seclusion of a monastery, which occupied the sites where the streets of Brompton, Earl's Court, Fulham, Walham Green, and Putney now stretch their interminable ramifications, and are accounted, justly enough, as London. Tell me, if you can, what are the bounds of London, north, south, east, or west. Does from Forest Gate on the east, to Richmond on the west, span its limits in one direction? and from Wood Green on the northern heights, to Croydon on the south, encompass it on the other? They may in this year of grace, but where will the boundary of continuous brick and mortar be set ten years hence? and where will then be the pleasant resorts of the present-day wheelman? They will all be ruined, and not, mark you, ruined from the commercial point of view, for the coming of the builder spells riches for the suburban freeholder, whose land, in the slang of the surveying fraternity, has become "ripe." These rustic places are, nevertheless, ruined from the point of view of the lover of the picturesque, and when he sees the old mansions going, the meadows trenched for foundations, and the lanes widened and paved by the newly constituted vestry, he groans in spirit. I am, for instance, especially aggrieved at the workings of modernity with Turnham Green.

I went to school there in the days when London was remote. We used to talk of "going up to London" then. Do any of the present-day inhabitants of Turnham Green, I wonder, speak thus? I imagine not. Turnham Green was then as rural as its name sounds now. The name, alas! is all that remains of its rurality, save, indeed, the two commons, the "Front" and "Back," as they are called. No one now remembers, I suppose, that the so-called "Back Common" is really Turnham Bec, even as the open space at Tooting remains Tooting Bec to this day. It is so, however, and it is only through this corruption that what is really and truly the original green of Turnham Green is dubbed the "Front Common." You see the humour of it?

THE NEW SUBURB

Turnham Green remained countrified until the railway came and took a slice off the so-called "Back Common," and built a station, and thus established the first outpost of Suburbia. Then another railway came, and took another slice, and a School Board filched another piece; and then great black boards, with white letters, began to be planted in the surrounding orchards, setting forth how "this eligible land" was to be let on building lease. Presently men who wore corduroys and waistcoats with sleeves to them, and leather straps round their trousers below the knees came along, and, with much elaborate profanity, built what were, with much humour, termed "villas" there. Streets of them, and all alike! After this, a tramway was made along the high-road, starting at Hammersmith, and ending at Kew Bridge. That tramway was amusing to us schoolboys, so long as the novelty of it lasted. Our school—it had the imposing name of Belmont House—faced the high-road, and it was our greatest delight of summer evenings to throw pieces of soap at the outside passengers of the trams from the bedroom windows. The expenditure of soap was tremendous, and sometimes those "outsiders" were hit, whereupon there was trouble! There was a gloomy old mansion opposite our school, called "Bleak House," and we used to think it was the veritable "Bleak House" of Dickens's story. We know better now. It still stands, but a furniture warehousing firm have built warehouses on to it, and it is no longer romantically gloomy.

IF ROBIN HOOD IS NOT AT HOME
TAKE A GLASS WITH LITTLE JOHN

ROBIN HOOD AND LITTLE JOHN.

The school has gone, too, where I learnt, and promptly forgot, Latin and Greek; and a row of shops, with big plate-glass windows and great gas lamps, have taken its place; and where we construed those dead (and deadly) languages, the linen-draper's assistant measures out muslins and calicoes. I have walked along these pavements during the last few days, and have noted more changes. There used to stand, beside the road, on the right hand as you go towards Gunnersbury, a little wayside "pub," with bow windows, and a bent and hunch-backed red-tiled roof. It was called the "Robin Hood," and an old-fashioned wooden post, supporting the swinging sign, stood on the kerb-stone, beside a horse-trough. I remember the sign well, for it had quite an elaborate picture painted upon it, representing Robin Hood and Little John. I can see quite clearly now that the artist of this affair obtained his ideas from the pictorial diplomas of the Ancient Order of Foresters; but, at the time, I thought it a very fine painting. The feathered hats impressed me very much indeed, although I always used to wonder why those two magnificent fellows hadn't pulled up their socks. It was some time before I discovered that they were not socks, but the big bucket boots of romance. They have pulled this old house down, and have built a glaring, flaring, gin-palace on the site of it, just as they did some five years ago to the old "Roebuck," not far off. The sign is gone, too, and wayfarers are no longer invited, if Robin Hood is not at home, to take a glass with Little John. What would happen, I often speculated, if both those heroes were away? Would, one take a glass, in that case, with Friar Tuck or Maid Marian?

THE "OLD WINDMILL."

OLD SUBURBAN INNS

There is an old inn still standing in this same high-road—most appropriately, by the way, situated next door to the Police Station, which, in its time, has extended hospitality to many a bold "road agent" who found his living on the Bath and Exeter Roads. The "Old Windmill" is a shy, retiring house which lies modestly some way back from the line of houses fronting the road. It has an open gravelled space in front, and a swinging sign on a post, which, together with an immense sundial on the front of the house, proclaims that the "Old Windmill" dates back to 1717. These are vestiges of the time when the Chiswick High Road was bordered by hedges instead of houses. The house, although it wears a certain old-world air, can scarce be called picturesque. The huge sundial just mentioned, with its mis-spelled legend, "So Fly's Life Away," gives it an interest, and so does the record of how one Henry Colam was arrested here one night toward the close of last century, on the charge, "For that he did molest and threaten certain of His Majesty's liege subjects upon the highway, in company with divers others, still at large." Henry had, as a matter of fact, "with divers others," attempted to rob the Bath Mail near this spot. He failed in his enterprise, but Bow Street had him all the same, and it does not require a very vivid imagination to conjure up a picture of his end.

Another old inn, which still stands at Turnham Green, although greatly altered, has a history not to be forgotten.

TREASON AND TREACHERY

At the "Old Pack Horse" (not by any means to be confounded with the "Pack Horse and Talbot," a quarter of a mile nearer on the road to London) assembled parties of the conspirators who, headed by their two principals, named, oddly enough, Barclay and Perkins,[1] plotted the assassination of King William the Third, on February 15, 1696. They were authorized by the exiled James the Second to do the deed, and had planned for forty of their band to surround the King's carriage as he returned from one of his weekly hunting expeditions from Kensington Palace to Richmond Park. His coach, they knew, would pass along a narrow, morass-like lane from the waterside on to Turnham Green, near where the church now stands, and they were well aware that, as it could at this point proceed only at a walking pace, William would fall an easy victim. It chanced, however, that there were traitors among their number, who informed the King's friends, so that on two succeeding Saturdays, while they were expecting him, he remained at Kensington. Many of the band were arrested, and six suffered the penalty of high treason.

The spot where the proposed assassination was to have been consummated is now known as Sutton Lane. At the corner of this suburban thoroughfare, where Fromow's Nursery stands, the fate of England was to have been decided.

THE "OLD PACK HORSE."

The "Old Pack Horse" has been somewhat modernized of late years by additions built out on the ground floor, but it remains substantially the same building at which Jack Rann, the famous "Sixteen-string Jack" of highway romance, may have taken a last drink with which to screw up his courage just before setting out to rob Dr. Bell, the chaplain to the Princess Amelia, in Gunnersbury Lane, near by. "Sixteen-string Jack" was hanged for that job in 1774.

He was peculiarly unfortunate, for Turnham Green and Gunnersbury were veritable Alsatias then, and those who travelled here should not have mentioned so ordinary a happening as having their purses taken. Indeed, it was so usual an occurrence that Horace Walpole tells us of a certain Lady Brown who, visiting here, always went provided with a purse full of brass tokens for the highwaymen. Imagination, conjuring up a picture of a Turpin or a Claude du Vall riding away with a pocketful of guineas which, on arriving home, he discovers to be counterfeits, provokes a smile.

XI

There are changes impending not far from here. Who that knows Kew Bridge has not an affection for that hump-backed old structure, although it presents many difficulties to the rider? Kew Bridge is doomed, and the powers that be are going to pull it down and build another in its stead—and one, it is almost unnecessary to add, not at all picturesque. Farewell, then, to the suburban delights of Kew. They are going to "improve" the river at Kew also—that river where, in summer time, the steamers get hung up on the sandbanks for lack of water. Alas, then, for the picturesque foreshore of Strand-on-the-Green!

KEW BRIDGE, LOW WATER.

HIGHWAYMEN

The passengers by the Bath Flying Machine grew at this point a shade paler. They generally expected to be robbed on Hounslow Heath, and their expectations were almost invariably realized by the gentlemen in cocked hats and crape masks, who were by no means backward in coming forward. The fine flower of the highwaymen practised on the Heath, and they did their spiriting gently and with so much courtesy that it was almost (not quite) a pleasure to hand over those rings and guineas of which so plenteous a store was collected every night.

Before, however, we come to Hounslow Heath, we have to cast a glance round Brentford, a town which holds the proud position of the county town of Middlesex. Foreigners might, in the innocence of their hearts, suppose that London would hold that honour; but to Brentford, known from time immemorial, and with the utmost justice, as "dirty Brentford," it has fallen. Has Brentford risen to the occasion? It must sorrowfully be admitted that it has not, and is a very marvel of dirt and dilapidation, and—But no matter! Until quite recently it also possessed, in the church of Old Brentford, the very ugliest church in England, which was so very ugly that it used to be credibly reported that people came long distances to see such a marvel of the unlovely. Alas! the church has been rebuilt, and so Brentford has lost a claim to distinction.

But Brentford has the honour of being mentioned in Shakespeare, in a passage whose allusions not all the efforts of antiquaries have been able to explain, and distinguished itself in a peculiar way during the reign of King William the Fourth, whom people used to call, for no very good reason, Silly Billy. The King and Queen were expected to drive through the town, on their way from Windsor to London, and the streets were decorated. But the inhabitants spiced their loyalty with sarcasm, for hanging on a line, stretched prominently across the road, was an old coat, turned inside out, in allusion to His Majesty's uncertain policy. Not satisfied, however, with this delicate way of calling him a turncoat, Brentford had another insult ready a little way down the street. The King was generally supposed to be very much under the influence of Queen Adelaide, and this was more or less gracefully alluded to by a pair of trousers fluttering in the wind like a banner suspended across the road. Their Majesties testified their recognition and appreciation of Brentford wit by never passing through the town again.

SORDID HOUNSLOW

A little further afield takes us to Hounslow, where John Jerry is busy putting up those long streets of "villas," whose deadly sameness vexes the soul of the artist. He has torn down the old houses, in one of which, or rather, in several of which—for they had intercommunicating passages—Dick Turpin was wont to hide when he was in refuge from the Bow Street runners.

"Bold Turpin vunce, on Hounslow Heath,
His mare, Black Bess, bestrod—er;
Ven there he see'd the bishop's coach
Coming along the road—er."

Thus sang Sam Weller; but "Bold Turpin" would be hard put to it to identify his suburban haunts now, and we, before our hair is grey, will find those places strange which were so familiar the matter of a few years ago.

COTTAGES, SUPPOSED TO HAVE BEEN THE HAUNTS OF DICK TURPIN.

The town of Hounslow is as unprepossessing as its name, which is saying a great deal. Its mile-long street, unlivened by any interesting features, is dull without descending to the positively interesting unloveliness of Brentford. Just as collectors prize old china whose shape and colouring are frankly hideous to those who are not of the elect in those matters, so the grotesquely dirty and ugly streets of Brentford have an interest for the tourist who does not often come upon their like. Hounslow's is just a commonplace ugliness. The curtailed remains of its once numerous and extensive coaching inns are become, as a rule, low pot-houses, in which labourers in the market-gardens that practically surround the town, sit and drink themselves stupid in the evening; and the business premises and private houses which alternate along the highway are either shabby old places, not old enough to claim any interest on the score of antiquity; or of a pretentious bad taste rather more difficult to bear with than the dirty hovels and tumbledown cottages they have displaced. Here, indeed, is the debateable ground between town and country. Rurality is (appropriately enough) in its last ditch, while civilization has established a precarious outpost beside it. Flashy "villas" jostle the market-gardeners' cottages; and respectability sits self-satisfied in its prim Early Victorian drawing-rooms, amid its chairs upholstered in green rep, its horsehair sofas and cut-glass lustres; while on either side the vulgar herd sits at open windows in its shirt-sleeves, and smokes black and exceedingly foul pipes, and gazes complacently upon the clothes hanging out to dry in the garden.

HOUNSLOW'S COACHING DAYS

Hounslow presented a different picture before the opening of the railways to the West. Two thousand post-horses were then kept in the town, and coaches and private carriages went dashing through at all hours of the day and night, so closely upon one another that they almost resembled a procession. As the poet says, the pedestrian then forced his way—

> "Through coaches, drays, choked turnpikes, and a whirl
> Of wheels, and roar of voices, and confusion;
> Here taverns wooing to a pint of 'purl,'
> There mails fast flying off, like a delusion."

And, indeed, they have, like delusions, vanished utterly. So early as April, 1842, a daily paper is found saying: "At the formerly flourishing village of Hounslow, so great is the general depreciation of property, on account of the transfer of traffic to the railway, that at one of the inns is an inscription, 'New milk and cream sold here;' while another announces the profession of the landlord as 'mending boots and shoes.'" The turnpike tolls at the same time, between London and Maidenhead, had decreased from £18 to £4 a week.

Yet Hounslow very narrowly missed becoming a great railway junction. That, indeed, was its proper destiny when the coaching era was done and the place decaying. Hounslow became the busy place it was in the days of road-travel, because it commanded the great roads to the West. The Bath and Exeter Roads, which were one from Hyde Park Corner as far as this town, branched at its western end, and it was also on the route to Windsor. It should thus have become an important station on the Great Western Railway, and might have been, had not other interests prevailed. It was the original intention of the Great Western directors, when the line was planned by Brunel in 1833, to keep close to the old high-road to Bath; but landed interests, both private and corporate, brought about numerous deviations, and so Hounslow was left to its fate, and the Great Western main line passes through Southall, two and a half miles distant, instead.

XII

We will now press on to the Heath, for our friends the highwaymen are anxiously awaiting us. Right away from the seventeenth century this spot bore a bad repute, when one of the most daring exploits was performed on its gloomy expanse. This was no less a feat than the plundering of that warlike general, Fairfax, by Moll Cutpurse. The most capable soldier of the age robbed by a woman highwayman, if you will be pleased to excuse the Irishry of the expression! But, indeed, the Roaring Girl, as her contemporaries called her, was the best man among the whole of that daring crew, and to her courage, her cunning, and her ready wit she owed the successful career that was hers. She wore the breeches in no metaphorical sense, but through all her career habited herself in man's garments. Only when she had amassed a fortune and had retired from "the road" did she don the skirt.

CLAUDE DU VALL

It is sad to think that the greatest of all the brotherhood who made Hounslow Heath and highway robbery synonymous terms was cut off in the full tide of his success. At least, it seems so to us, although the travellers of the period doubtless felt a certain satisfaction when Du Vall was executed, on January 21, 1670. He was but twenty-seven years of age, and already had become a star of the first magnitude. He was, in fact, a master of the whole art and mystery of robbing upon the road, and to this he brought the most perfect courtesy. Violence had no part in the methods of this artist, and he would have scorned, we may be sure, the ruffianly and even murderous acts of a later generation of the craft, which not only despoiled travellers of their goods, but rendered the Heath dangerous to life and limb. His chief exploit is classic, and is set forth so eloquently, and with such an engaging profusion of capital letters, in a contemporary pamphlet, that one cannot do better than quote it:—

"He, with his Squadron, overtakes a Coach which they had set over Night, having Intelligence of a Booty of four hundred Pounds in it. In the Coach was a Knight, his Lady, and only one Serving-maid, who, perceiving five Horsemen making up to them, presently imagined that they were beset; and they were confirmed in this Apprehension by seeing them whisper to one another, and ride backwards and forwards. The Lady, to shew that she was not afraid, takes a Flageolet out of her pocket and plays. Du Vall takes the Hint, plays also, and excellently well, upon a Flageolet of his own, and in this Posture he rides up to the Coachside. 'Sir,' says he to the Person in the Coach, 'your Lady plays excellently, and I doubt not but that she dances as well. Will you please to walk out of the Coach and let me have the Honour to dance one Currant with her upon the Heath?' 'Sir,' said the Person in the Coach, 'I dare not deny anything to one of your Quality and good Mind. You seem a Gentleman, and your Request is very reasonable.' Which said, the Lacquey opens the Boot, out comes the knight, Du Vall leaps lightly off his horse and hands the Lady out of the Coach. They danced, and here it was that Du Vall performed Marvels; the best Masters in London, except those that are French, not being able to shew such footing as he did in his great French Riding Boots. The Dancing being over (there being no violins, Du Vall sung the Currant himself) he waits on the Lady to her coach. As the knight was going in, says Du Vall to him, 'Sir, you have forgot to pay the Musick.' 'No, I have not,' replies the knight, and, putting his Hand under the Seat of the Coach, pulls out a hundred Pounds in a Bag, and delivers it to him, which Du Vall took with a very good grace, and courteously answered, 'Sir, you are liberal, and shall have no cause to repent your being so; this Liberality of yours shall excuse you the other Three Hundred Pounds,' and giving the Word, that if he met with any more of the Crew he might pass undisturbed, he civilly takes his leave of him. He manifested his agility of body by lightly dismounting off his horse, and with Ease and Freedom getting up again when he took his Leave; his excellent Deportment by his incomparable Dancing and his graceful manner of taking the hundred Pounds."

When this hero had gone the inevitable way of his fellows, he was buried with great pomp and circumstance in the church of St. Paul, Covent Garden, with a set of eulogistic verses for his epitaph. Unfortunately, the old church was destroyed by fire and the epitaph with it.

HIGHWAY MURDERS

Mr. Nuthall, the Earl of Chatham's solicitor, too, who had been to Bath to confer with his gouty and irascible client, was stopped in his carriage as it was going towards London across this dreaded wilderness. The highwaymen fired at him, and he died of fright. Two other notable murders by highwaymen took place here—in 1798 and 1802—and bear witness to the degeneracy of the craft. The first was Mr. Mellish, who was fired upon and killed as he was returning from a run with the King's hounds. A Mr. Steele was the other victim, and his assailants, Haggarty and Holloway, who had planned the crime at the "Turk's Head," Dyot Street, Holborn, it is satisfactory to be able to add, were hanged. The execution took place at the Old Bailey, when twenty-eight persons among the crowds who had come to see the sight were crushed to death. Up to the year 1800, the Heath was a most famous place for gibbets. "The road," as a writer of the period says, "was literally lined with gibbets on which the carcases of malefactors hung in irons, blackening in the sun." Du Vall had a successor in Twysden, Bishop of Raphoe, collecting tithes in rather a promiscuous way, by turning highwayman in 1752. His career was a short one, for one of the first travellers he bade "Stand!" on the Heath shot him through the body, from which he died a few days later, at the house of a friend, from "inflammation of the bowels," as the contemporary report, jealous for the reputation of the dignified clergy, put it.

Shall I weary you by recounting more of these highway crimes? There was Dr. Shelton, a surgeon, who flourished in the early thirties of last century, and, deserting lancet and scalpel, took to the road and that not more lethal weapon, the horse-pistol; though, to be sure, it was more for show than use, for not Du Vall himself could have been more courteous.

That the poet who wrote of Bagshot Heath as a place "where ruined gamblers oft repay their loss" might with perfect propriety have substituted "Hounslow" will be readily seen when we mention Parsons, nearly contemporary with Shelton, who robbed at Hounslow that he might gamble in London. Parsons was the son of a "Bart. of the B.K.," as the Tichborne Claimant would have phrased it; an Eton boy, at one time an officer both in the Army and Navy, and the husband of a beautiful heiress. He made an edifying end at Tyburn.

Then there was Barkwith, a mere novice, whose first sally led to a like exit. He was the son of a Cambridgeshire squire, and manager to a Lincoln's Inn solicitor. He had "borrowed" trust moneys wherewith to satisfy some debts of honour; and so the hour of four o'clock in the afternoon of a November day found him on the Heath, with a pistol in his hand and his heart in his mouth, "holding up" a coach. The booty was but a miserable handful of silver; but, being captured, he died for it, all the same. Let us trust he did "the young gentlemen who belong to Inns of Court" an injustice when, in his dying speech and confession, he warned his hearers against them as "the most wicked of any."

"DARE-DEVIL SIMMS"

Then there was Dare-devil Simms—"Gentleman Harry," as his friends called him—a midshipman who came up from deserting his ship in the West Country. First borrowing a saddle and bridle, and then stealing a horse, he commenced his career by robbing a post-chaise and the Bristol Mail, and coming to London, soon became a noted figure on this stage. One night he relieved a Mr. Sleep of his purse. The despoiled traveller bewailed his loss bitterly, but Harry comforted him with the assurance that he would have been robbed in any case; if not by himself, certainly by one or other of the two who were waiting for him down the road. "But if you meet them," said he, "sing out 'Thomas!' and they will let you pass." The unfortunate man went on his way calling "Thomas!" to every one he met, and narrowly escaped being severely handled by some gentlemen who conceived themselves insulted.

Presently Tyburn claimed Gentleman Harry also, and a career which had been begun by transportation, and continued through such stirring adventures as being sold for a slave, becoming a sailor and a privateersman, was finally extinguished by the halter. A short life and a merry.

Strawkins, Simpson, and Wilson, too, helped to keep up the stirring story of the road. They intercepted the Bristol Mail and left the postboy, bound with ropes, at the bottom of a ditch on the outskirts of Colnbrook. They were tracked down by the Post Office, and, Wilson turning King's evidence, the first two were hanged. The Mail was then given an escort of Dragoons, but highway robbery had too strong a spice of adventure for one of these fine fellows to resist it. He accordingly pillaged the Bath Stage, and suffered the appointed end in due course.

This catalogue of mine does not close until 1820, in which year four confederates plundered the Bristol Mail. They had booked the inside seats, and during their journey through the night forced open the strong boxes placed under the seats, decamped with their contents, and were never heard of again.

XIII

A STORY OF THE ROAD

One of the most diverting stories of Hounslow Heath, which serves to relieve its sombre repute, is that which the late Mr. James Payn tells, in one of his reminiscences. "The story goes," he says, "that early in the century the landlord of Skindle's, at Maidenhead, was a strong Radical, and could command a dozen votes; but his prosperity had a sad drawback in the person of his son, a good-for-naught. During a certain Berkshire election, a Tory solicitor was staying at this inn, and had occasion to go to London for the sinews of war. His gig was stopped on his way back, on Hounslow Heath, by a gentleman of the road.

"I have no money," said the lawyer, with professional readiness, "but there is my watch and chain."

"You have a thousand pounds in gold in a box under the seat," was the unexpected reply; "throw back the apron!"

The lawyer obeyed, but as the horseman stooped to take the box, the lawyer knocked the pistol out of his hand and drove off at full gallop. He had a very quick-going mare, and before the highwayman could find his weapon, which had fallen into some furze, was beyond pursuit.

The next morning the lawyer sent for the landlord. "Yesterday," he said, "I was stopped on Hounslow Heath. The man had a mask on, but I recognized him by his voice, which I can swear to. I knew him as well as he knew me. You had better speak to your son about it, and then we will resume our conversation."

The landlord was quite innocent of his son's intended crime, but he had reason to believe him capable of it. He went out with a heavy heart, and when he came back his face showed it. "Well," he said, with a sort of calm despair, "what steps do you intend to take, sir, in the matter?"

"None to hurt an old friend, you may be sure," answered the lawyer; "only those twelve votes you boasted about must be given to our side instead of yours;" which was accordingly arranged.

In those days, as will already have been seen, Hounslow Heath was a very real place indeed. There was (as the journalistic slang of to-day has it) "actuality" about that then solitary and barren waste, which is not a little difficult to realize nowadays. The cyclist who speeds over the level roads and past the smiling orchards and market gardens, finds it difficult to believe that this was the sinister place of eighty years ago; and, since there is no Heath to-day, is apt to come to the conclusion that it must have been the very "Mrs. Harris" of heaths; a figment, that is to say, of romantic writers' imaginations. Such, however, was by no means the case. Where cultivated lands are now, and where suburban villas stand, there stretched, less than eighty years since, a veritable scene of desolation. Furze-bushes, swampy gravel-pits in which tall grasses and bulrushes grew, and grassy hillocks, the homes of snipe and frogs, and the haunts of the peewit, were the features of the scene by day; while, when night was come, the whole place swarmed with footpads and highwaymen.

LORD BERKELEY'S ADVENTURES

At that time Lord Berkeley used frequently to stay at his country house at Cranford, close by, from Saturdays to Mondays, and had twice been stopped and robbed on his way before a third and last encounter, in which he shot his assailant dead. On the second occasion, the door of his travelling carriage was opened, and a footpad, dressed as a sailor, pointed a fully-cocked pistol at him. The man's hand trembled violently, and while my lord was producing what money he had about him, the trigger was pulled, more, it would seem, from accident than intention. Happily, the pistol missed fire. The man then exclaimed, "I beg your pardon, my lord," and, recocking his pistol, retreated with his plunder.

After this escape, Lord Berkeley swore he would never be robbed again, and always travelled at night with a short carriage-gun and a brace of pistols. Thus armed, it was on a November night in 1774 that he was attacked for the last time. He was going to dine with Mr. Justice Bulstrode, who lived in an old house surrounded by a brick wall, near where Hounslow's modern church now stands, and as the carriage was nearing the town, a voice called to the postboy to halt, and a man rode up to the carriage window on the left-hand side, thrusting in a pistol, as the glass was let down. With his left hand Lord Berkeley seized the weapon and turned it away, while with his right he pushed the short double-barrelled gun he had with him against the robber's body, and fired once. The man was severely wounded, and his clothes were set on fire, but he managed to ride away some fifty yards, and then fell dead. Two accomplices then appeared, but Lord Berkeley, and a servant on horseback who rode behind the carriage, made for them, and they fled. It was then discovered that the gang were all amateur highwaymen, and youths from eighteen to twenty years of age, in good positions in London.

The Earl of Berkeley seems to have been somewhat unduly twitted about this encounter. Society was quite resigned to seeing highwaymen hanged, although it made heroes of them while they were waiting in the "stone jug" at Newgate for that fatal morning at Tyburn; but it appears to have considered the shooting of one of them an unsportsmanlike act.

Lord Chesterfield, however, should have been quite the last man to sneer at the Earl on this score, for he himself was under a very well-deserved public censure for having prosecuted Dr. Dodd, his son's tutor, for forgery, with the result that the Doctor was hanged. Accordingly, when he sarcastically asked Lord Berkeley "how many highwaymen he had shot lately," it is pleasing to record that he was readily reduced to silence by the retort, "As many as you have hanged tutors; but with much better reason for doing so."

XIV

CRANFORD

It is just beyond Cranford Bridge that the pumps which are so odd a feature of the Bath Road begin. They line the highway on the left-hand side going from London, and are all situated in the same position as shown in the illustration. They are of uniform pattern, and are placed at regular intervals. These pumps are relics of the coaching age, but are peculiar to the Bath and some stretches of the Exeter roads. Placed here for keeping the highway well watered in the old days of road-travel, they have evidently long been out of use; in fact, their handles are all chained up. They recur so regularly that they might almost form part of a new table of measurement, as thus:—

63 paces	equal	1 telegraph-post.
19 telegraph-posts	"	1 mile.
2 miles	"	1 pump.
1½ pumps	"	1 pub.

A BATH ROAD PUMP.

Cranford is a more picturesquely romantic place than any one has a right to expect in the Middlesex of these latter days. That outlying portion of the village which borders the high-road still wears the air of a tentative settlement of civilization amid the wilds of the rolling prairie, and might form a ready object-lesson for any untravelled Englishman who desires "local colour" for the writing of an American romance in the *genre* of Bret Harte. And, indeed, the houses grouped around Cranford Bridge were, some seventy years ago, built on the very borders of Hounslow Heath, whose dreary and dangerous wastes only found a boundary here, beside the still waters of the placid Crane. At Cranford Bridge stands that fine old coaching inn, the "Berkeley Arms," and opposite the "White Hart," which must have been in those times very havens of refuge in that wild spot; and away up the lane to the right hand lies the village and park, as pretty a spot as you shall find in a long day's march. Cranford village is rich in beautiful old mansions set in midst of walled gardens whose formal precincts are entered through massive wrought-iron gates. Beside this lane is the village "lock-up," or "round-house," built in 1810, and now the only one of its kind left anywhere near London. The rest have all been demolished, but "once upon a time" no village could have been considered complete without one, or without the whipping-post and stocks which were generally erected close at hand. Cranford, of course, being situated in the midst of the alarums and excursions caused by the highwaymen who infested the vicinity and kept the inhabitants in a state of terror every night, had a peculiarly urgent need for such a place, and it is, perhaps, because those gentry were such expert prison-breakers, that this example is more than usually strong, the door being plated with iron, and the small square window filled with sheet iron pierced with small holes.

THE "BERKELEY ARMS."

CRANFORD ROUND HOUSE

Cranford Park, near by, was a seat of the Earls of Berkeley, and is now the residence of Lord Fitzhardinge, who is *de facto* "Earl of Berkeley." But the romantic scandals which arose from the fifth Earl having eventually married a servant in his household, after she had borne him several children, caused so much litigation about the succession to the title that, although one of his sons, the Hon. Thomas Moreton Fitzhardinge-Berkeley, was declared by a decision of the House of Lords to be legitimate, he never assumed the title, for the reason that the barring of his elder brother reflected upon his mother's good name. The whole affair is exceedingly involved and mysterious, and it is therefore quite in order that Cranford House should have the reputation of being haunted.

The house is a large rambling pile in the midst of the Park, overlooking the sullen ornamental waters formed from the river Crane. The ancient parish church stands close by. The chief or garden front of the house is curiously like one of the old-fashioned houses that give so distinctive a character to Park Lane, in London; having a double-bayed front with verandahs. The aspect of such a house standing in the open country is weird in the extreme.

CRANFORD HOUSE.

THE CRANFORD GHOST

It was the Hon. Grantley Berkeley who first drew attention to the "haunted" character of the house. He tells, in his "Recollections," how one night when he and his brother had returned home late, they went down into the kitchen in search of some supper, all the rest of the household having retired to rest long before, and distinctly saw the tall figure of an elderly woman walk across the kitchen. Thinking it was one of the maids, they spoke to her, but she vanished into thin air, and a search discovered nothing at all. The obvious comment here is that people returning home late at night in those times very frequently saw things that had no existence. The narrator's father, however, used to describe how he saw a man in the stable-yard, and thinking he was some unauthorized visitor in the Servants' Hall, asked him what he was doing there. The man "vanished" without a reply; to which the rejoinder may well be made that he might do so and yet be no ghost; the motive force being a sight of the horsewhip which the Earl was carrying.

Cranford deserves notice from the literary pilgrim from the circumstance that Dr. Thomas Fuller, the Fuller of the much-quoted "Worthies of

England," was chaplain to George, Lord Berkeley, who presented him to the rectory in 1658. He lies buried in the chancel of the church.

Harlington Corner is the name of the spot, half a mile down the road, where one of the many old roadside hostelries stands by a branch road leading on the right to Harlington, and on the left to East Bedfont, on the Exeter Road. The Corner, besides leading to Harlington, was also the "junction" for Uxbridge, and here the slow stages set down or took up passengers for that town. The fast coaches did not stop here, or were supposed not to do so. Some of them, however, in defiance of time-bills, halted at the "Magpies"— by arrangement, of course, with the innkeeper—much to the profit of that house. One of these venal drivers was neatly caught by Mr. Chaplin, of the once well-known coaching firm of Chaplin and Horne. The coachman had with him on the box seat that day a particularly genial passenger, who proved also to have a very intimate knowledge of horseflesh. Pulling up at the "Magpies," where tables were spread, showing that the coach was expected as a matter of course, he winked at his passenger and invited him to refresh. Then, when all was, as the poet would say, "merry as a marriage-bell," the unknown, like another "Hawkshaw the Detective," revealed himself. He was Chaplin! The coachman drove that coach no more!

THE "OLD MAGPIES."

"ARLINGTON OF HARLINGTON"

Harlington, up the road to Uxbridge, was once the seat of the Bennets, one of whom, Henry Bennet, was created Viscount Thetford and Earl of Arlington in 1663, and lives in history as the "Arlington" of the Cabal. He selected this village for one of his titles, but the 'eralds' College (as it surely should have been called) made out his patent of nobility without the "H," and so "Arlington" he had to become. Arlington Street, Piccadilly, remains to this day, and the Dukes of Grafton, in whose numerous titles this is merged, are still Barons "Arlington of Harlington, in Middlesex."

After which we will hasten on, passing Sipson (a corruption of "Shepiston") Green. Here we come upon the trail of messieurs the footpads again, for the road between this inn and the humbler "Old Magpies," a few hundred yards further on, is sad with the story of highway murder.

XV

The times of the highwaymen are, fortunately for the wayfarer, if unhappily for romance, long since past, and many of the once-notorious haunts of Sixteen-string Jack, Claude du Vall, Dick Turpin, and their less-famed companions have disappeared before the ravages of time and the much more destructive onslaughts of the builder. A hundred years ago it would have been difficult to name a lonely suburban inn that was not more or less favoured and frequented by the "Knights of the Road." Nowadays the remaining examples are, for those interested in the old story of the roads, all too few.

Perhaps this queer little roadside inn, the "Old Magpies," is the most romantic-looking among those that are left. For one thing, it possesses a thick and beetle-browed thatch which impends over the upper windows like bushy eyebrows, and gives those windows—the eyes of the house—just that lowering and suspicious look which heavy and bristling eyebrows confer upon a man.

But it is not only its romantic appearance that gives the "Old Magpies" an interest, for it is a well-ascertained fact that outside this house, so near to the once terrible Hounslow Heath, the brother of Mr. Mellish, M.P. for Grimsby, was murdered by highwaymen in April, 1798, when returning from a day's hunting with the King's hounds.

He had started with two others from the "Castle" Hotel, at Salt Hill, for London, after dinner, and the carriage in which the party was seated was passing near the "Old Magpies" at about half-past eight, when it was attacked by three footpads. One held the horses' heads while the other two guarded the windows, firing a shot through, to terrify the occupants. They then demanded money. No one offered any resistance, purses and bank-notes being handed over as a matter of course. Then the travellers were allowed to go, a parting shot in the dark being fired into the carriage. It struck Mr. Mellish in the forehead. Coming to another inn near by, called the "Magpies," the wounded man was taken upstairs and put to bed, while a surgeon was sent for.

He came from Hounslow, and was robbed on the way by the same gang. Additional medical assistance was called in, but this late victim of highway robbery died within forty-eight hours.

SIR JOSEPH BANKS

The assassins were never apprehended, although Bow Street sent its cleverest officers to track them down. Bow Street caught the smaller fry readily enough, who snatched handkerchiefs and such petty booty, and hanged them out of hand, while the more desperate villains generally escaped. This is not to say that the Bow Street Runners were not vigilant and zealous. Indeed, their zeal sometimes outran their discretion, as instanced in their bold capture of Sir Joseph Banks, who was collecting natural history specimens in the wilds. Sir Joseph, distinguished man of science though he was, and a gentleman, was singularly ill-favoured, and in this fact lies the chief sting of Peter Pindar's witty verses on the subject—

"Sir Joseph, fav'rite of great Queens and Kings,
Whose wisdom weed- and insect-hunter sings;
And ladies fair applaud, with smile so dimpling;
Went forth one day amid the laughing fields
Where Nature such exhaustless treasure yields—A-simpling!
It happened on the self-same morn so bright
The nimble pupils of Sir Sampson Wright,
A-simpling too, for plants called Thieves, proceeded;
Of which the nation's field should oft be weeded."

They seize Sir Joseph.

"'Sirs, what d'ye take me for?' the Knight exclaimed—
'A thief,' replied the Runners, with a curse;
'And now, sir, let us search you, and be damn'd'—
And then they searched his pockets, fobs, and purse,
But, 'stead of pistol dire, and death-like crape,
A pocket-handkerchief they cast their eye on,
Containing frogs and toads of various shape,
Dock, daisy, nettletop, and dandelion,
To entertain, with great propriety,
The members of his sage Society;
Yet would not alter they their strong belief
That this their pris'ner was a thief.

"'Sirs, I'm no highwayman,' exclaimed the Knight—
'No—there,' rejoined the Runners, 'you are right—
A footpad only. Yes, we know your trade—
Yes, you're a pretty babe of grace;
We want no proofs, old codger, but your face;
So come along with us, old blade.'
……
"Sir Joseph told them that a neighb'ring Squire
Should answer for it that he was no thief;
On which they plumply damn'd him for a liar,
And said such stories should not save his beef;

>   And, if they understood their trade,
>   His *mittimus* should soon be made;
>   And forty pounds be theirs, a pretty sum,
>   For sending such a rogue to Kingdom Come."

To the Squire, however, they took that distinguished member of Society, who, of course, identified him at once, and bade them beg his pardon. This they did—according to "Peter Pindar"—with a resolution in future not to judge of people by their looks!

XVI

Just before reaching the roadside hamlet of Longford, fifteen miles from Hyde Park Corner, a lane leads on the right hand to Harmondsworth, a short mile distant across the wide flat cabbage and potato fields. "Harm'sworth," as the rustics call it, is mentioned in Domesday Book, under the name of "Hermondesworde;" that is to say, Hermonde's sworth or sward, the pasture-land of some forgotten Hermonde.

THE "GOTHIC BARN"

Few ever turn aside from the dusty high-road to visit this old-fashioned village, rich in old timber-framed houses, and possessing an ancient tithe-barn which, standing next the church, was once part of an obscure Priory established here. The "Gothic Barn" is built precisely on ecclesiastical lines, with nave and aisles, and is the largest of the tithe-barns now remaining in England, being 191 feet in length and 38 feet, in breadth. The walls are built of a rough kind of conglomerate found in the locality, and called "pudding-stone," the flints and pebbles distributed through the rock resembling to a lively imagination the currants and raisins in plum-puddings. The interior of the barn is a vast mass of oak columns and open roofing.

THE "GOTHIC BARN," HARMONDSWORTH.

A relic of old country life may be seen hanging in this barn, in the shape of a flail, now occasionally used for threshing out beans.

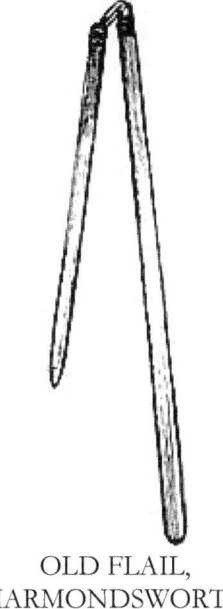

OLD FLAIL,
HARMONDSWORTH

Very few people will understand the meaning of the old English word "flail," because it is almost fifty years since that old-world agricultural implement was in general use. Until steam was introduced as a labour-saving appliance in agricultural work, corn was invariably threshed out of the ear by wooden instruments like that pictured here, consisting of two unequal lengths of rounded wood of the size of an ordinary broomstick, connected by leathern loops.

The farm hands who used this primitive contrivance grasped hold of the longer stick, and, brandishing it about over their heads, brought the hinged end down repeatedly on the wheat spread out on the threshing floor; thus, with the expenditure of considerable time and muscular strength, separating the grains from the ears. As the "business end" of the flail is constructed so as to swing in every direction, it is obvious that the mastery of it was only acquired with practice, and at the cost of sundry whacks on the head brought on himself by the clumsy novice. Indeed, it is an instrument requiring particular dexterity in manipulation.

Longford obtains its name from the marshy ford over one of the sluggish branches of the Colne, which anciently spread over the road at this spot. The ford was eventually replaced by the bridge, called "Queen's Bridge," which now carries the highway over the stream close by the old inn now called the "Peggy Bedford," from a well-remembered landlady who kept the house in coaching days, and died in 1859. The real name of it, however, now almost forgotten, is the "King's Head." The spot is picturesque in the grouping of gnarled old wayside trees with the quaint house and its luxuriant garden; and more so, perhaps, because it comes as a surprise from the hitherto unrelieved monotony of the flat road all the way from Cranford Bridge.

COLNBROOK

In another mile and three-quarters the road reaches Colnbrook, in midst of whose long street one of the numerous channels of the Colne divides the counties of Middlesex and Bucks. The boundaries of English counties are rarely marked for the information of wayfarers along the highways and byeways of the country, but here the brick bridge over the Colne, built in 1777, has inscriptions which mark where the frontiers march together; and when the Bath Road is crowded with cyclists on Saturday afternoons in summer-time one or more can generally be found standing on the bridge with one leg in each county.

There are no fewer than four channels of the Colne here, and the land all round about is flat and waterlogged. The entrance to Colnbrook from London is in fact quite a little Holland in appearance, where streams flow sluggishly beside the road and are spanned by many footbridges that give access to the gardens of the pleasant country cottages on either side. A fine avenue of elms shades the road, and ahead is the cramped street of Colnbrook with its mellowed red-brick houses and bright red-tiled roofs. Colnbrook street is narrow to a degree, and it is surprising how the many coaches that used to come tearing through at all hours of day and night managed to escape accidents. There is reason for this narrowness, for Colnbrook was originally built upon a stone causeway across the marshes of the Colne, and nowhere else were there to be found solid foundations. The original causeway may possibly have been Roman, for this is said to have been the station of *Ad Pontes*, described by Antoninus in his *Itineraries*. Staines, however, is more likely the site of it.

THE COUNTY BOUNDARY.

THE "OSTRICH"

Colnbrook is probably the best example of a decayed coaching-town now to be found in the Home Counties. Too remote from London for suburban expansion to have affected it, the quaint street remains much as it was a hundred, nay two hundred years ago. The last coach might have left yester-year, so undisturbed appears to be the place. There are coaching-inns here of vast size, ranging from the solid-looking "George" with "eighteenth century" proclaimed plainly enough on its stolid face, back to the "Ostrich," rambling, gabled, timber-framed, Elizabethan. They would have you believe that this house stands on the site of one of the old guesthouses established in the eleventh, twelfth, and succeeding centuries along the roads by the good Churchmen of those times. The original guesthouse here, however, appears to have been a secular foundation, for it is recorded that in 1106, a certain Milo Crispin gave it—"*quoddam hospitium in viâ Londoniæ apud Colebroc*"—to the Abbot of Abingdon. The sign of the "Ostrich" is therefore a lineal descendant of "*Hospitium*," *viâ* "Hospice" and "Ospridge;" for, as we have already seen, the letter H has ever been a negligeable quantity.

The original house is said by persistent traditions to have been the scene of a dreadful series of abominable murders something of the "Sweeny Todd" order. The West of England, even so far back as five hundred years ago, was famous for its cloth, and along this road, with their bales and pack-horses, journeyed the rich clothiers to and from the London market, halting in their tedious travels at the inns on the way. The "Ostrich" was one of these, and prospered exceedingly by the patronage of those jolly merchants. The gold they carried, however, aroused the cupidity of the innkeeper and his wife, who devised a murder-trap in one of the upstairs bedrooms, by which the bed, which was placed above a trap-door, was tilted up in the middle of the night, so that its slumbering occupant was shot into a huge copper of boiling water, and so scalded to death. According to this tradition, which itself is some hundreds of years old, thirteen victims were thus disposed of, and the innkeeper waxed rich. There must have been other accomplices, for, according to the story, the bodies were kept until they formed a cartload, when they were heaped up, driven away to the Thames at Wraysbury and thrown in. One, however, had fallen out by the way, and whilst the criminals were disputing by the river-bank as to what had become of it, they were observed by a fisherman who had been hidden in the rushes while engaged in setting eel-bucks. He suggested that the best thing for them to do was to throw in one of themselves, to make up the number; to which sprightly wit they replied with a shower of arrows. The fisherman then rowed away, with one of the arrows sticking in his boat, and went with it into Colnbrook the following day. Outside the "Ostrich" he was espied by the innkeeper's little son, who exclaimed, "You have got one of my father's arrows!" The man and his wife were missing, but were afterwards captured and hanged.

COLNBROOK, A DECAYED COACHING TOWN.

This gory legend does not render Colnbrook the more attractive to the stranger, but the Colnbrook folks are proud of it. Like the Fat Boy in "Pickwick," they "wants to make yer flesh creep," and would have one believe that the present "Ostrich" is the identical building—which it isn't.

Another cherished tradition of Colnbrook is that King John stayed here on his journey to Runneymede to sign the famous Magna Charta, the "Palladium of English Liberties," as phrase-makers are pleased to call it. They still show the stranger "King John's Palace," a quaint house which looks on to the road, and is not so old as John's time by some three hundred years. That, however, by no means discredits the story to the good folks of Colnbrook.

A better ascertained historical event is the rising in favour of the deposed Richard the Second in 1400, when forty thousand men from the West Country lay encamped by the Colne, prepared to descend upon Windsor and London, to seize the usurper, Henry the Fourth. But Henry, fleeing from Windsor, raised an army in London; and between the rumours of his coming and treachery in their own ranks, the partisans of Richard faded away.

XVII

TO SLOUGH

The long stretches of the Bath Road between this and Slough are nowadays enlivened by few incidents or interesting places, although during the last century, and well on into this, the highway was lively enough with Royalties and their escorts, journeying between Windsor and St. James's. The route taken on these occasions was generally through Datchet, and so on to the Bath Road just here. An old print of this period shows us how George the Third used to travel on this road to London, or to the unkingly domestic life at Kew Palace, where the farmer-like reputation of that not very brilliant monarch was sustained on boiled mutton and turnips, and improving books.

ALMSHOUSES, LANGLEY.

The hamlet of Langley Broom, one and a half miles on the way, is the uninteresting offshoot, of the pretty village of Langley Marish (or "Marshy Langley"), that lies just within sight of the road, and has some delightful old red-brick almshouses, which, together with the ancient library and painted room of Renaissance period in the church, render the place worthy a visit.

This is all there is to interest the stranger, with the exception of a pretty peep towards Windsor Castle on the left hand, within two miles of Slough, and near where Cary of the *Itinerary* places a spot he calls "Tetsworth Water," which does not appear to exist nowadays.

THE STOLEN FOUNTAIN.

A STOLEN FOUNTAIN

Slough is quite modern and unremarkable, but it is rapidly building up legends of its own. There have, for instance, been many strange thefts on the roads, from time to time, but none perhaps stranger than the purloining, two years ago, of the drinking-fountain which used to stand at the entrance to Slough, where the road branches off to Uxbridge. Until some unusually acquisitive folk came along and carried it away with them, there was at that corner a fountain of bronze and marble, fourteen feet in height, the bronze upper part weighing nearly half a ton. It acted also as a finger-post, directing strayed cyclists in the way they should go. The good folks of Slough went to bed one night and saw their fountain standing where it had been used to stand for years past; but in the morning, when they arose and went forth about their business, the fountain was gone! Nothing but the plinth was left. Some mad wag suggested that one of the many cyclists who frequent the Bath Road had taken it home with him as a memento of Slough; but it seems that a gang of original-minded thieves made away with it for the sake of the bronze, which, when broken up, must have brought them a good sum. At any rate, it seems quite beyond the bounds of possibility that Slough will ever see its fountain again.

WINDSOR CASTLE, FROM THE ROAD NEAR SLOUGH.

XVIII

It requires the specialized knowledge of a district surveyor to determine where Slough ends and Salt Hill begins, although probably it would be a shrewd guess to say that the roads which cross the Bath Road in the midst of Slough, and go respectively left and right to Windsor and Stoke Poges, form the dividing line. For all practical purposes, however, the places are one. Salt Hill has decayed, rather than grown, while the town of Slough (unlovely name!) is almost wholly a creation of the railway. Not only strangers have noted the unpleasing name of the place, but some of the inhabitants even endeavoured to change it a few years ago. The proposition was to rechristen it "Upton Royal," Upton being a hamlet near by, the "Royal" a bright idea of the local boot-lickers, who wanted to emphasize the fact of their proximity to Windsor. The project fell through.

A TRAGICAL DINNER

Many of the crack coaches halted at Salt Hill, where, at the "Castle" or the "Windmill," they found accommodation of the very best. Salt Hill, in fact, was a place which thrived solely on coaching, and the glories of it are now departed. A tragical event clouded over the fair fame of the "Castle" in 1773. It seems that on the 29th of March in that year, a number of gentlemen forming the Colnbrook Turnpike Commission met there, when the Hon. Mr. O'Brien, Capt. Needham, Edward Mason, Major Mayne, Major Cheshire, Walpole Eyre, Capt. Salter, Mr. Isherwood, Mr. Benwell, Mr. Pote, senr., and Mr. Burcombe attended and dined together. The dinner consisted of soup, jack, perch, and "eel pitch cockt" (whatever that may have been), fowls, bacon, and greens, veal cutlets, ragout of pigs' ears, chine of mutton and salad, course of lamb and cucumbers, crawfish, pastry, and jellies. The wines were Madeira and Port of the very best quality; but, notwithstanding this elaborate spread, the company, we are told, ate and drank moderately, nor was there excess in any respect. Before dinner, several paupers were examined, and among them one most remarkably miserable object. In about ten or eleven days afterwards, every one of the company, except Mr. Pote, who had walked in the garden during the examination of the paupers, was taken ill, and five of them soon died. It was, at the time, supposed that some infection from the paupers had occasioned this fatality, more especially as Mr. Pote, who was absent from the examination, was the only person who escaped unaffected, although he had dined in exactly the same manner as the others.

Some persons have compared this affair with the mortality arising from the Black Assizes, but it should seem, by another account, that these unfortunate gentlemen had partaken of soup that had been allowed to stand in a copper vessel, and that, therefore, they died of mineral poisoning. They lie buried in the little churchyard of Wexham, two miles distant, where an inscription records the facts. That sad business quite ruined the "Castle" Hotel.

But all the Salt Hill hotels were ruined when the Great Western Railway was constructed. The first section was opened, from Paddington to Taplow, on June 4, 1838, and those old hostelries at one blow found most of their patrons taken from them. It is true that this disaster had been impending since 1833, when the route for the new railway was first surveyed; but after the victory of the opponents of the first Bill, when a public meeting was held at Salt Hill to rejoice in the defeat of the railway project, the innkeepers seemed to think that they could not come to much harm. They were, however, bitterly disillusioned.

OPENING OF THE G.W.R.

It is curious, nowadays, to look back upon the time when the Great Western Railway was first built. The authorities of Eton College, together with the Court, had effectually driven the railway from Windsor and Eton, and the College people had also secured the insertion of a clause in the Company's Act forbidding the erection of a station at Slough. Notwithstanding this, however, trains stopped at Slough from the very first. The Company did this by an ingenious evasion of the spirit, if not the letter, of their Parliamentary obligations. By their Act they were forbidden to *build a station* at Slough, but nothing had been said about trains stopping there! Accordingly, two rooms were hired at a public house beside the line where Slough station now stands, and tickets were issued there, comfortably enough. The Eton College authorities were maddened by this smart dodge, and applied for an injunction against the Company, which was duly refused.

This is not the only railway romance belonging to Slough, for the Slough signal-box has had a romance of its own. The cabin was erected in 1844, and one of the earliest messages the signalman wired to London by the then wonderful new invention of the electric telegraph, was intelligence of the birth of the Duke of Edinburgh. The following year a man named Tawell committed a murder at Salt Hill, and escaped by the next train to London; but information was telegraphed to town, and being arrested as he stepped from the carriage at Paddington, he was subsequently tried and hanged. The telegraphist warned the officials at Paddington to look out for a man dressed like a Quaker. It is a singular circumstance that the original telegraphic code did not comprise any signal for the letter "Q;" but the telegraphist was not to be beaten. He spelled the word "Kwaker." Sir Francis Head has recorded how he was travelling along the line, months after, in a crowded carriage. "Not a word had been spoken since the train left London, but as we neared Slough Station, a short-bodied, short-necked, short-nosed, exceedingly respectable-looking man in the corner, fixing his eyes on the apparently fleeting wires, nodded to us as he muttered aloud, "Them's the cords that hung John Tawell!"[2]

XIX

It will not surprise those who are acquainted with the history of Bath, and the crowds of rich travellers who travelled thither, to learn that Hounslow Heath had not long been left behind before another highwayman's territory was entered upon. This stretched roughly from Salt Hill, on the east, to Maidenhead Thicket, on the west. It would, of course, have been ill gleaning after the harvest had been reaped by the pick of the profession on the Heath, and, as a matter of fact, the gangs who infested Maidenhead Thicket and Salt Hill confined their attention to travellers *returning* from Bath. Hawkes was the chief of them, and his was a name of dread.

THE "FLYING HIGHWAYMAN"

Hawkes, the "Flying Highwayman," who obtained that eminently descriptive name from the rapidity with which he moved from place to place, levying tribute from the frequenters of the Bath Road, was a darkly prominent figure in the days of George the Third. His name perhaps is not so well known as that of the more than half-mythical Dick Turpin, but it deserves especial mention from the circumstance of his keeping the whole country side between Hounslow and Windsor in terror for some years, and from the cleverness of the disguises he assumed. Disguised now as an officer, or a farmer; or again, as a Quaker, he despoiled the King's liege subjects very effectively. His most notable exploit was enacted at Salt Hill.

A vapouring fellow, apparently from the sister island, who, according to his own account of his antecedents, had been too frequently in action with hosts of enemies to care for footpads and such scum, alighting from a post-chaise, entered the wayside sign of the Plough, and laying down a pair of large horse-pistols, called loudly for brandy-and-water.

Only one guest was in the room—a broad-hatted and drab-suited Quaker—who, in the most sedate manner, was satisfying his appetite with a modest meal. The traveller, swaggering in and laying down his weapons on the table in such close proximity to the edibles, startled the man of peace, who shrank from them in very terror.

"Oh, my friend," says the traveller, "'tis folks who fear to carry arms give opportunities to the highwaymen. If they went protected as I do, what occasion would there be to fear any man, even Hawkes himself?" And then, with an abundance of oaths, he protested that not half a dozen highwaymen should avail to deprive him of a single sixpence. The Quaker, meanwhile, continued his humble refection, now and again glancing from his bread and cheese at his most noisy and demonstrative companion, who drank his brandy-and-water stalking up and down the apartment.

Presently, his drink exhausted, and his eloquence thrown away upon friend Broadbrim—who he at once conceived to be so quiet because he had nothing to lose—he unceremoniously turned his back and sat down upon a chair to examine the valuables he carried about his person. Having satisfied himself of their safety, he snatched up his pistols, and, with an impatient exclamation, strode off to the bar, and was paying for his liquor and gossiping, when the silent Quaker, who had by this time finished his repast, passed out hurriedly and disappeared down the road.

THE HIGHWAYMAN AND HIS PREY

The boisterous traveller continued his conversation for a while with the landlord, and then, re-entering his post-chaise, bade the postboy drive fast, and holloa when a suspicious person approached. He threw himself upon the seat after he had closed the door, stretched his legs as wide as possible, and, planting his feet firmly, cocked his pistols, holding them at arm's length with their barrels resting on the open windows.

The horses went on for about a mile, when the chaise entered upon a heath—a very desolate-looking place, with never a house visible in any direction: with nothing, indeed, to enliven the perspective save a gallows, if such an object, with a rattling skeleton swinging in chains from the cross-beam, can be so considered. The traveller gazed with a grim satisfaction at this spectacle, for it seemed to him, as to the shipwrecked sailor in the old story—an earnest of civilization.

But while he was musing on the long arm of the law, the rapid sounds of horse's hoofs, sounding over the ragged turf of the heath, were heard, and a voice was presently raised, commanding the postboy to stop. The chaise was stopped suddenly, with a jolt and a crash, and a face, black-masked, mysterious, horrible, appeared at the window, together with the still more alarming apparition of the grinning muzzle of a horse-pistol. Then followed the inevitable, "Your money or your life!"

The traveller had his weapons ready. Raising the muzzle of one to the highwayman's head, he pulled the trigger, while his unexpected assailant stood and laughed. Beyond a snap and some sparks from the bruised flint, nothing happened. With a curse, he levelled the other pistol, and with the same result. The man in the mask laughed louder. "No good, friend Bounce, trying that game," said he, coolly; "the powder was carefully blown out of each of thy pans, almost under thy nose. If thou dost not want a bullet through thy head, just hand me over the repeater in thy boot, the purse in thy hat, the bank-notes in thy fob, the gold snuffbox in thy breast, and the diamond ring up thy sleeve. Out with them," he added, "in less time than thee took when I saw thee put 'em there, or I'll send thee to Davy Jones, and take 'em myself."

The muzzle of the highwayman's pistol was at his head—the trigger at full cock. The flashing eyes that sparkled behind the mask showed the unfortunate traveller that here was no man to be trifled with. He dropped his useless weapon, and with considerable trepidation drew, one by one, from their places of security the valuables mentioned by the highwayman, who, when he had received them all, drew half a crown from the purse, and, flinging it into the chaise, said, casting off his Quaker speech, "There is enough to pay your turnpikes. And, harkee!" he added, in a more peremptory tone, "for the future, don't brag quite so much." Turning his horse's head, he disappeared, leaving the chaise and its occupant to continue their journey. The latter speedily recognized that the Quaker was none other than Hawkes himself.

AN ALE-HOUSE FIGHT

But this was the last exploit of Captain Hawkes. On the evening of the same day a man in a heavy topcoat and riding-boots, splashed, and with every appearance of having come off a long journey, entered the "Rising Sun," at a village about twenty miles away. In one compartment of the tap-room, on either side of a painted table, sat two ploughmen, in smock-frocks, their shock heads resting on their arms, which were spread out on the table near an empty quart pot. They were both snoring loudly. The new-comer, having been served with a glass of gin and water, and a long clay pipe, took no notice of the sleepers. In a few minutes one of the rustics awoke, and, glancing vacantly about him, scratching his carroty head, seized the empty pot.

He put it down, and, giving his companion a push that nearly sent him off his seat, exclaimed, "Ye greedy chap! blest if ye ain't been and drunk up all the beer while I were a-sleeping."

"Then ye shouldn't have been a-sleeping, ye fool," retorted the other, grinning from ear to ear.

"I'll gi' ye a dowse o' the chaps if ye grin at me," shouted the man, angrily.

"Haw, haw!" jeered the grinner, across the table. "'Twould take a better man nor you to do it. And," he added, "if ye don't want a hiding, ye'd better not try."

Up jumped the two chawbacons simultaneously, and rushed at one another furiously. They rolled on the sanded floor, kicking and cuffing, while the stranger sipped his gin and water and smoked placidly enough.

Presently, however, one of the combatants opened a clasp-knife, and made as though he would stab the other. Seeing this, the quiet spectator rose and seized the man's wrist in a powerful grip. But, quick as thought, his own wrists were seized, and he was thrown to the floor, both men clinging tightly to him. When he at length managed to rise, both his wrists were handcuffed.

"Neatly managed, that!" exclaimed one of the pretended rustics, throwing off his smock-frock and disclosing the red waistcoat of a Bow Street Runner.

"You must acknowledge, Captain Hawkes, as how we've done you brown."

They searched their captive, and found two loaded pistols and a great variety of valuables about him. Then they escorted him to a post-chaise, which was in waiting; and the same night saw him in Newgate.

He made a quiet and composed end, like most of his kind. They knew their risks, these dauntless enemies of society, and accepted death by strangulation when it came with something of philosophy.

XX

And now for the plain, unvarnished narrative of one who travelled these roads a century ago.

A STRANGER IN OUR GATES

When that simple-minded German, Pastor Moritz, who visited England towards the close of last century, grew tired of London, he determined, he says, to visit Derbyshire; and, making the necessary preparations for his excursion, set out on June 21, 1782, for Richmond, though why he should have gone to Richmond *en route* for Derbyshire is difficult to understand. He took with him four guineas, some linen, and a book of the roads, together with a map and a pocket-book, and (for he had his appreciations) a copy of "Paradise Lost."

Thus equipped, he enjoyed for the first time what he calls the "luxury of being driven in an English stage," from which expression and our own people's doleful tales of eighteenth-century travelling in England, we may infer that the public conveyances of the Pastor's native land were particularly bad. The English coaches were, according to him, viewing them with the eye of a foreigner, "quite elegant." This particular one was lined in the inside, and had two seats large enough to accommodate six persons; "but it must be owned," he goes on to say, "that when the carriage was full the company was rather crowded." By which we may gather that the seats rather discommoded than accommodated.

The only passenger at first was an elderly lady, but presently the coach was filled with other dames, who appeared to be a little acquainted with one another, and conversed, as our traveller thought, in a very insipid and tiresome manner. Fortunately, he had his road-book handy, and so took refuge in its pages by marking his route.

The coach stopped at Kensington, where a Jew would have taken a seat, but that luxurious conveyance was full inside, and the Israelite was too proud to take a place amongst the half-price outsiders on the roof. This naturally annoyed the travellers, for they thought it preposterous that a Jew should be ashamed to ride on the outside. They thought he should have been grateful for being allowed to ride on any side in any way, since he was but a Jew. In this connection Mr. Moritz takes occasion to observe that the riding upon the roof of a coach is a curious practice. Persons to whom it was not convenient to pay full price sat outside, without any seats, or even a rail. By what means passengers thus fastened themselves securely on the roofs of those vehicles he knew not, but he constantly saw numbers seated there, at their ease, and apparently with perfect safety.

On this occasion the outsiders, of whom there were six, made such a noise and bustle when the insiders alighted, as to almost frighten them, and I suspect the ladies were rendered horribly nervous by the only other man who rode inside the coach recounting to them all kinds of stories about robbers and footpads who had committed many crimes hereabouts. However, as this entertaining companion insisted, the English robbers were possessed of a superior honour as compared with the French: the former robbed only; the latter both robbed and murdered, doubtless on the principle of that classic proverb which assures us that dead men tell no tales.

THE HIERARCHY OF THIEVES

"Notwithstanding this," says our traveller, "there are in England another species of villains, who also murder, and that oftentimes for the merest trifles, of which they rob the person murdered. These are called footpads, and are the lowest class of English rogues, amongst whom, in general, there reigns something like some regard to character.

"The highest order of thieves (!) are the pickpockets or cutpurses, whom you find everywhere, and sometimes even in the best companies. They are generally well and handsomely dressed, so that you take them to be persons of condition; as indeed may sometimes be the case—persons who by extravagance and excesses have reduced themselves to want, and find themselves obliged at last to have recourse to pilfering and thieving.

"Next to them come the highwaymen, who rob on horseback, and often, they say, even with unloaded pistols, they terrify travellers in order to put themselves in possession of their purses. Among these persons, however, there are instances of true greatness of soul; there are numberless instances of their returning a large part of their booty where the party robbed has appeared to be particularly distressed, and they are seldom guilty of murder.

"Then comes the third and lowest and worst of all thieves and rogues, the footpads before mentioned, who are on foot, and often murder in the most inhuman manner, for the sake of only a few shillings, any unfortunate people who happen to fall in their way."

The coach arrived, one is glad to say, unharmed at Richmond, despite forebodings of disaster; but the pirates on board (so to speak) demanded another shilling of the Pastor, although he had already paid one at starting.

At Richmond he stayed the night, and in the evening he took a walk out of the town, to Richmond Hill and the Terrace, where his feelings during the few enraptured minutes that he stood there seemed impossible for his pen to describe. One of his first sensations was chagrin and sorrow for the days wasted in London, and he vented a thousand bitter reproaches on his irresolution in not quitting that huge dungeon long before, to come here and spend his time in paradise.

The landlady of the inn was so noted for the copiousness and the loudness of her talking to the servants that our traveller could not get to sleep until it was very late; but, notwithstanding this, he was up by three o'clock the next morning to see the sun rise over Richmond Hill. Alas! alas! the lazy servants, who cared nothing for such sights, did not arise till six o'clock, when he rushed out, only to be disappointed at finding the sky overcast.

And now, having finished his breakfast, he seized his staff, his only companion, and proceeded to set forth on foot. Unfortunately, however, a traveller in this wise seemed to be considered as a sort of wild man or eccentric creature, who was stared at, pitied, suspected, and shunned by all. There were carriages without number on the road, and they occasioned a troublesome and disagreeable dust, and when he sat down in a hedge to read Milton, the people who rode or drove past stared at him with astonishment, and made significant gestures, as who should say, "This is a poor devil with a deranged head," so singular did it appear to them that a man should sit beside the public highway and read books.

PILGRIM'S PROGRESS

Then, when he again resumed his journey, the coachmen who drove by called out now and again to ask him if he would not ride on the outside of their coaches; and the farmers riding past on horseback said, with an air of pity, "'Tis warm walking, sir;" and, more than all, as he passed through the villages, every old woman would come to her door and cry pitifully, "Good God!"

And so he came to Windsor, where, as he entered an inn and desired to have something to eat, the countenances of the waiters soon gave him to understand that they thought our pedestrian little, if anything, better than a beggar. In this contemptuous manner they served him, but, to do them justice, they allowed him to pay like a gentleman. "Perhaps," says Pastor Moritz, "this was the first time these pert, be-powdered puppies had ever been called on to wait on a poor devil who entered the place on foot." To add to this indignity, they showed him into a bedroom which more resembled a cell for malefactors than aught else, and when he desired a better room, told him, with scant ceremony, to go back to Slough. This, by the way, was at the "Christopher," at Eton. Crossing the bridge into Windsor again, he found himself opposite the Castle, and at the gates of a very capital inn, with several officers and persons of distinction going in and out. Here the landlord received him with civility, but the chambermaid who conducted him to his room did nothing but mutter and grumble. After an evening walk he returned, at peace with all men; but the waiters received him gruffly, and the chambermaid, dropping a half-curtsey, informed him, with a sneering laugh, that he might go and look for another bedroom, for the one she had by mistake shown him was already engaged. He protested so loudly at this that the landlord, who was a good soul, surely, came, and with great courtesy desired another room to be shown him, which, however, contained another bed.

Underneath was the tap-room, from which ascended the ribaldries and low conversation of some objectionable people who were drinking and singing songs down there, and scarcely had he dropped off to sleep before the fellow who was to sleep in the other bed came stumbling into the room. After colliding with the Pastor's bed, he found his own, and got into it without the tiresome formality of removing boots and clothes.

The next morning the Pastor prepared to depart, needlessly annoyed by that eternal feminine—the grumbling chambermaid, who informed him that on no account should he sleep another night there. As he was going away, the surly waiter placed himself on the stairs, saying, "Pray remember the waiter," and when in receipt of the three-halfpence which our traveller bestowed, he cursed that inoffensive German with the heartiest imprecations. At the door stood the maid, saying, "Pray remember the chambermaid." "Yes, yes," says the Pastor (a worm will turn), "I shall long remember your most ill-mannered behaviour," and so gave her nothing.

Through Slough he went, by Salt Hill, to Maidenhead. At Salt Hill, which could hardly be called a village, he saw a barber's shop. For putting his hair in order, and for the luxury of a shave, that unconscionable barber charged one shilling.

Between Salt Hill and Maidenhead, this very much contemned pedestrian met with a very disagreeable adventure. Hitherto he had scarcely met a single foot-passenger, whilst coaches without number rolled every moment past him; for few roads were so crowded as was the Bath Road at this time.

THE PASTOR AND THE FOOTPAD

In one place the road led along a low, sunken piece of ground, between high trees, so that one could see but a little way ahead, and just here a fellow in a brown frock and round hat, with an immense stick in his hand, came up to him. His countenance was suspicious. He passed, but immediately turned back and demanded a halfpenny to buy bread, for he had eaten nothing (so he said) that day.

The Pastor felt in his pocket, but could find nothing less than a shilling. Very imprudently, I should say, he informed the beggar of that fact, and begged to be excused.

"God bless my soul!" said the beggar, which pious invocation so frightened our timid friend that he, having due regard to the big stick and the brawny hand that held it, gave the beggar a shilling. Meanwhile a coach came past, and the fellow thanked him and went on his way. If the coach had come past sooner, he "would not," he says, "so easily have given him the shilling, which, God knows, I could not well spare. Whether a footpad or not, I will not pretend to say; but he had every appearance of it."

And so this unfortunate traveller marches off to the Oxford Road, and we are no longer concerned with him.

XXI

A fine broad gravel stretch of highway is that which, on leaving Salt Hill, takes us gently down in the direction of the Thames, which the Bath Road crosses, over Maidenhead Bridge. The distance is four miles, with no villages, and but few scattered houses, on the way. Two miles and one mile respectively before the Bridge is reached are the wayside inns, called "Two Mile Brook" and "One Mile House." Near this last is the beautiful grouping of roadside elms, sketched in the accompanying illustration, "An English Road." Half a mile onward, the Great Western Railway crosses the road by a skew-bridge, and runs into Taplow station. Taplow village lies quite away from the road, but has an outpost, as it were, in the old, with the curious sign of the "Dumb Bell." Beyond this, the intervening stretch of road as far as Maidenhead Bridge is lined with villas standing in extensive grounds. Here the traveller renews his acquaintance with the Thames, and passes over a fine stone bridge, built in 1772, from Bucks to Berks. This bridge succeeded a crazy timber structure, which itself had several predecessors. It is one of these early bridges that is mentioned in the declaration of a hermit who obtained a licence to settle here and collect alms. Such roadside hermits were common in the Middle Ages. They were licensed by the Bishop of their diocese, and were often useful in keeping bridges and highways in good order; the alms they received being, indeed, very much in the nature of voluntary tolls for these services. On the following declaration, Richard Ludlow obtained his licence:—

AN EARLY TOLL-KEEPER

"In the name of God, Amen. I, Richard Ludlow, before God and you my Lord Bishop of Salisbury, and in presence of all these worshipful men here being, offer up my profession of hermit under this form: that I, Richard, will be obedient to Holy Church; that I will lead my life, to my life's end, in sobriety and chastity; will avoid all open spectacles, taverns, and other such places; that I will every day hear mass, and say every day certain Paternosters and Aves: that I will fast every Friday, the vigils of Pentecost and All Hallows, on bread and water. And the goods that I may get by free gift of Christian people, or by bequest, or testament, or by any reasonable and true way, receiving only necessaries to my sustenance, as in meat, drink, clothing, and fuel, I shall truly, without deceit, lay out upon reparation and amending of the bridge and of the common way belonging to ye same town of Maidenhead."

AN ENGLISH ROAD.

There is, perhaps, no more delightful picture along the whole course of the Bath Road than the view from Maidenhead Bridge up river, where the houseboats, gay with flowers and Japanese lanterns, are gathered beside the trim lawns of the riverside villas, with the gaily dressed crowds by Boulter's Lock beyond, and the wooded heights of Clieveden closing in the distance. Maidenhead shows the river at its most fashionable part.

It was at the "Greyhound" Inn, Maidenhead, that the unhappy Charles the First bade farewell to his children, July 16, 1647. He was in charge of his Roundhead captors at Caversham, and had been allowed to come over for two days. The Prince of Wales was abroad, but the Duke of York, then fifteen years of age; the Princess Elizabeth, two years younger; and the seven-year-old Duke of Gloucester, were brought to him. The affecting scene is said to have drawn tears even from Cromwell.

Maidenhead Bridge—the wooden one which preceeded the present structure—might have been the scene of a desperate encounter, but happened instead to have witnessed an equally desperate and farcical devil-take-the-hindmost flight on the part of the Irish soldiers of James the Second, who were posted here to dispute the passage of the Thames with the advancing forces of William of Orange.

The November night had shrouded the river and the country side, when the sound of drums beating a Dutch march was heard. The soldiers, who had no heart in their work, did not remain to defend that strategic point, and bolted. They would have discovered, if they had kept their posts, that the martial music which lent them such agility was produced by the townsfolk of Maidenhead, who, in spite of that national crisis, appear to have been merry blades.

XXII

The "Bear" was the principal inn at Maidenhead in the coaching era, and owed much of its prosperity to the unwillingness of travellers who carried considerable sums of money with them to cross Maidenhead Thicket at night. They slept peacefully at the "Bear," and resumed the roads in the morning, when the highwaymen were in hiding.

MAIDENHEAD THICKET

Maidenhead Thicket is really a long avenue lining the highway two miles from that town. It is a beautiful and romantic place, but its beauties were not apparent to travellers in days of old. The sinister reputation of the spot goes back for hundreds of years, and may be said to have arisen from the time of the Dissolution of the Monasteries, when Reading Abbey was despoiled. To that Abbey had resorted many hundreds of poor, certain of finding relief at its gates, and when its hospitality had become a thing of the past, these dependents simply infested the neighbourhood, and either begged or stole. As a chronicler of that time quaintly said: "There is great stoare of stout vagabonds and maysterless men (able enough for labour) which do great hurt in the country by their idle and naughtie life." In those times the Hundreds were liable for any robberies committed within their boundaries; and in 1590 the Hundred of Benhurst, in which Maidenhead Thicket is situated, had actually to pay £255 compensation for highway robberies committed here. In fact, Maidenhead Thicket had for a long time an unenviable reputation for highway robberies, with or without violence, and the desperadoes had so little care whom they robbed that not even the Vicars of Hurley, who came over to officiate at Maidenhead once a week, were safe. This was so fully recognized that the Vicars of Hurley used to draw an annual £50 extra on account of their risks.

In later years a farmer, whose name was Cannon, was stopped one night on driving from Reading market. Two footpads compelled him to give up the well-filled money-bag he carried with him, and then let him go, consumed with impotent rage at his helplessness and the loss of his money.

Suddenly, however, he remembered that he had with him, under the seat of the gig, a reaping-hook which he had brought back from being mended at Reading. That recollection brought him a bright idea. Turning his gig round, he drove back to the spot where he had been robbed, by a back way. As he had supposed, the ruffians were still there, waiting for more plunder. In the dark they took the farmer for a new-comer, until he had got to close quarters with his reaping-hook, which they mistook for a cutlass. The end of the encounter was that one footpad was left for dead, and the other took to his heels. The farmer searched the fallen foe and found his money-bag, together, it was said, with other spoils, which he promptly annexed, and drove off rejoicing.

MAIDENHEAD THICKET.

After these tales of derring-do and robustious encounters, the story of the road becomes comparatively tame as it goes on and passes through Twyford and Reading.

THE "BELL AND BOTTLE" SIGN.

"BELL AND BOTTLE"

At the western end of Maidenhead Thicket, where, lying modestly back from the road, stands one of the innumerable "Coach and Horses" of the highway, the gossips of the adjacent Littlewick Green foregather and play bowls on the grass. Then comes Knowl Hill, where an old sign, swinging romantically from a wayside fir tree, proclaims the proximity of a curiously named inn, the "Bell and Bottle." What affinity have bells for bottles, or bottles for bells? "What," as the poet asks (in quite a different connection), "is Hecuba to him, or he to Hecuba?" But perhaps the original innkeeper was something of a cynic, and thus paraphrased the well-worn conjunction, "Beer and Bible." Unfortunately for the inquiring stranger, the origin is "wrop in mistry."

Down below Knowl Hill, past a chalk quarry on the right, is yet another inn—the neat and pretty "Seven Stars," to be succeeded at the hamlet of Kiln Green by the "Horse and Groom," gabled and embowered with vines, and facing up, not fronting, the road, in quite the ideal fashion. What the country here lacks in bold scenery it evidently gains in fertility, for the gardens of Kiln Green are a delightful mass of luxuriant flowers.

The road through Hare Hatch to Twyford is flat and uninteresting. Twyford itself, an ancient place on the little river Loddon, is losing its antique character, from being the scene of much building activity. An old almshouse remains on the right hand, with the inscription, "Domino et pauperibus, 1640."

The five miles between Twyford and Reading exhibit the gradual degeneracy of a country road approaching a large town; as regards the scenery, that is to say. The quality of the road surface remains excellent, and the width is generous—a circumstance probably owing to the especial widening carried out so far back as 1255, in consequence of the dangerous state of the highway, which was then narrow and bordered by dense woods wherein lurked all manner of evildoers.

Three miles from the town, and continuing for the length of a mile, is a pleasant avenue of trees. The deep Sonning Cutting on the Great Western Railway is then crossed, and the suburbs of Biscuit Town presently encountered.

XXIII

"The run to Reading," I learn from a cycling paper, "constitutes a pleasant morning's spin from London." I should like to call up one of our great-grandfathers who travelled these thirty-nine miles painfully by coach, and read that paragraph to him.

BISCUITS, SEEDS, AND SAUCE

Reading numbers over 60,000 inhabitants, and is rapidly adding to them. This prosperity proceeds from several causes, Reading being—

> "'Mongst other things, so widely known,
> For biscuits, seeds, and sauce."

The town, of course, stands for biscuits in the minds of most people, and the names of Huntley and Palmer have become household words, somewhat eclipsing Cock's Reading Sauce, and the seeds of Sutton's; while few people outside Reading are cognizant of its great engineering industries. So much for modern Reading, whose principal hero is George Palmer.

PALMER'S STATUE.

Mr. George Palmer, whose death occurred in 1897, enjoyed the distinction of having a statue erected to him during his lifetime, an unusual honour which he shared with few others—Queen Victoria, the great Duke of Wellington, Lord Roberts, Reginald, Earl of Devon, and, of course, Mr.

Gladstone. Mr. Palmer's fellow-townsmen elected to honour him in this way, and decided to have a statue which should be in every way true to life, and show the man "in his habit as he lived"—one in which the clothes should be as characteristic as the features. Our grandfathers would have represented him wrapped in a Roman toga, but those notions do not commend themselves to the present age, and so the effigy stands in all the supremely *un*-decorative guise of everyday dress: homely coat, and trousers excruciatingly baggy at the knees; bareheaded, and in one hand a silk hat and an unfolded umbrella. This is possibly the only instance in which these last necessary, but unlovely articles have been reproduced in bronze.

Ancient Reading knew nothing of biscuits or sauces. It was the home of one of the very greatest Abbeys in England. The Abbot of Reading ranked next after those of Westminster and Glastonbury, and usually held important offices of State. In the Abbey, Parliaments have been held, Royal marriages celebrated, and Kings and Queens laid to rest. Yet of all this grandeur no shred is left. There are ruins; but, formless and featureless as they are, they cannot recall to the eye anything of the architectural glories of the past, and the bones of the Kings have for centuries been scattered no man knows whither.

There are pleasant stories of Reading, and gruesome ones. Horrible was the fate of Hugh Faringdon, the last Abbot, who was, in 1539, with one of his monks, hanged, drawn and quartered for denying the religious supremacy of that royal wild beast, Henry the Eighth. The King had been friendly with him not so long before, and had presented him with a silver cup, as a token of this friendship.

THE KING AND THE ABBOT

One wonders if this unfortunate prelate was the same person as that Abbot of Reading mentioned by Fuller. The Abbot of that story was a man particularly fond of what have been gracefully termed the "pleasures of the table." His eyes, as the Psalmist puts it, "swelled out with fatness,"—and his stomach, too, for that matter. To him came one day a hungry stranger, fresh from the appetizing sport of hunting. He had lost his way, and craved the hospitality of the Abbey. That hospitality was extended to him, promptly enough, and he was seated at the Abbot's own table.

It will readily be guessed that this hungry stranger was the King. He had wandered thus far, away from Windsor Forest and his attendants, and was genuinely famished. The Abbot, however, had no notion who he was; but he could see that this strayed huntsman was a very prince among good trencher-men, and envied him accordingly. "Well fare thy heart," said he, as he saw the roast beef disappearing; "I would give an hundred pounds could I feed so lustily on beef as you do. Alas! my weak and squeezie stomach will hardly digest the wing of a small rabbit or chicken."

The King took the compliment and more beef, and, pledging his host, departed. Some weeks after, when the Abbot had quite forgotten all about the matter, he was sent for, clapped into the Tower, and kept, a miserable prisoner—not knowing what his offence might be, or what would befall him next—on bread and water. At length one day a sirloin of beef was placed before him, and he made such short work of it as to prove to the King, who was secretly watching him, that his treatment for "squeezie stomach" had succeeded admirably; so, springing out of the cupboard in which he had secreted himself, "My lord," says he, "deposit presently your hundred pounds in gold, or else you go not hence all the days of your life. I have been your physician to cure you, and here, as I deserve, I demand my fee for the same."

The Abbot was enlightened. He, as Fuller says, "down with his dust, and, glad he escaped so, returned to Reading, as somewhat lighter in purse, so much more merry in heart, than when he came thence."

Little remains at Reading to tell of the coaching age. Where are the "Bear," the "George," the "Crown"? Gone, with their jovial guests, into the limbo of forgotten things, almost as thoroughly as the civilization of Roman Calleva—the Silchester of modern times—situated at some distance down the road from Reading to Basingstoke, and whose relics may be seen gathered together in the Reading Museum. To that collection should be added a set of articles used in the everyday business of coaching. They would be just as curious to-day as those Roman potsherds of a thousand years ago.

XXIV

The Bath Road climbs, with some show of steepness, out of Reading, presently to enter upon that stretch of nearly seventeen miles of comparatively flat sandy gravel road which, for speed cycling, is the best part of the whole journey. The surface is nearly always splendid, save in very dry seasons, when the sand renders the going somewhat heavy, and the cyclist may well be surprised to learn that it was here, between Reading and Newbury, that Pepys and his wife, travelling in their own coach, lost their way, entirely through the badness of the roads.

THE STAGE WAGGON. (*After Rowlandson.*)

THE "BERKSHIRE LADY"

In spite of these modern advantages, the road is quite suburban and uninteresting until Calcot Green is passed, in two miles and a half. But it is here, amid the pleasant, though tame, scenery that Calcot Park, the home of the famous "Berkshire Lady," may be sought.

The "Berkshire Lady" was the daughter of Sir William Kendrick, of Calcot, who flourished in the reign of Queen Anne. Upon the death of her father, she became sole heiress to the estate and an income of some five thousand pounds per annum. Rich, beautiful, and endowed with a vivacious manner, it is not surprising that she was courted by all the vinous, red-faced young squires in the neighbourhood; but she refused these offers until, according to an old ballad—

> "Being at a noble wedding
> In the famous town of Reading,
> A young gentleman she saw
> Who belonged to the law."

We may shrewdly suspect that she not only "saw" him, but that they indulged in a desperate flirtation in the conservatory, or what may have answered to a conservatory in those times.

The "Berkshire Lady" was evidently a New Woman, born very much in advance of her proper era. For what did she do? Why, she fell in love with that "young gentleman" straight away, and so furiously that nothing would suffice her but to send him an anonymous challenge to fight a duel or to marry her.

Benjamin Child—for that was the name of the young and briefless (and also impecunious) barrister—was astonished at receiving a challenge from no one in particular; but, accompanied by a friend, proceeded to the rendezvous appointed by the unknown in Calcot Park. Arrived there, they perceived a masked lady, with a rapier, who informed the pair that she was the challenger:—

> "'It was I that did invite you:
> You shall wed me, or I'll fight you,
> So now take your choice,' said she;
> 'Either fight, or marry me.'
> Says he, 'Madam, pray what mean ye?
> In my life I ne'er have seen ye;
> Pray unmask, your visage show,
> Then I'll tell you, aye or no.'"

The lady, however, would not unmask:—

> "'I will not my face uncover,
> Till the marriage rites are over;
> Therefore take you which you will,
> Wed me, sir, or try your skill.'"

The friend advised Benjamin Child, Esq., to take his chance of her being poor and pretty, or rich and—plain (those being the usually accepted conjunctions), and to marry her, which he accordingly promised to do. He had a reward for his moral courage, for the lady unmasked and disclosed herself as the beautiful unknown with whom he had flirted at the wedding. That they "lived happily ever afterwards" we need find no difficulty in believing.

THEALE.

Many stories were current locally of this Mr. Child. One, in particular (certainly not a romantic one), related his great fondness for oysters, of which he was in the habit of consuming large quantities; in fact, he is said to have kept a museum of the tubs emptied by him, for one room in Calcot House was fitted round with shelves, upon which these empty mementos were arranged in regular order. It was his humour to show his friends this unique arrangement as a convincing proof of his capabilities in that particular branch of good living.

Upon the death of his wife, Calcot became unbearable to him, and he sold it. But, curiously enough, nothing could induce him to quit the house, and the new proprietor was reduced to rendering it uninhabitable to him by unroofing it. Mr. Child then retired to a small cottage in an adjoining wood, where he spent the rest of his days in retirement.

The Kendrick vault in the church of St. Mary, Reading, was exposed to view in 1820, when, among the numerous coffins found, was one bearing the inscription, "Frances Child, wife of Benjamin Child, of Calcot, first daughter of Sir W. Kendrick, died 1722, aged 35." The coffin was of lead, and was moulded to the form of the body, even to the lineaments of the face. Mr. Child was the last person buried in this vault. His coffin, of unusually large dimensions, is dated 1767.

THEALE

Two and a half miles from Calcot Green, and we are at Theale, a village prettily embowered among trees, but possessing a large and extraordinarily bad "Carpenter's Gothic" church, built about 1840, which looks quite charming at the distance of a quarter of a mile, but has been known to afflict architects who have made its close acquaintance with hopeless melancholia. In fine, Theale church is a horrid example of Early Victorian imitation of the Early English style.

And now the road wanders sweetly between the green and pleasant levels beside the sedgy Kennet. Road, rail, river, and canal run side by side, or but slightly parted, for miles, past Woolhampton and the decayed town of Thatcham, to Newbury, and so on to Hungerford.

A short mile before reaching Woolhampton, there stands, on the left-hand side of the road, quite lonely, a wayside inn, the "Rising Sun," a relic of coaching times. They still show one, in the parlour, the old booking-office in which parcels were received for the old road-waggons that plied with luggage between London and Bath, and talk of the days when the house used to own stabling for forty horses. A larger inn is the "Angel," at Woolhampton, with a most elaborate iron sign, from which depends a little carved figure of a vine-crowned Bacchus, astride his barrel, carved forty years ago by a wood-carver engaged on the restoration of Woolhampton Church. Tramps and other travellers unacquainted with the classics generally take this vinous heathen god to be a representation of the Angel after whom the inn was named.

WOOLHAMPTON.

Woolhampton, once blessed with two "Angels," has now but one, for what was once known as the "Upper Angel" has been re-named the "Falmouth Arms." Although Woolhampton village possesses a railway station on the Hants and Berks branch of the Great Western Railway, travellers will look in vain for the name of it in their railway guides. If they will refer to "Midgham," however, they will have found it under another title. Originally called by the name of the village, it was found that passengers and luggage frequently lost their way here in mistake for Wolverhampton, also on the Great Western, and so the name had to be changed.

THATCHAM.

THATCHAM

Three and a half miles from Woolhampton comes Thatcham, famed in the coaching age for its "King's Head" inn, but now a decayed market town which has sunk to the status of a very dull village. A battered stone, all that remains of a market cross, stands in the middle of the wide, deserted street, enclosed by a circular seat, bearing an inscription recounting the history of the market, and the kingly protection which Henry the Third afforded the place against the "Newbury men." But, kingly help notwithstanding, the "Newbury men" have long since snatched its trade away from Thatcham, which has become a village, while Newbury has grown to be a town of 20,000 inhabitants. The only interesting object in the long street is Thatcham Chapel, an isolated Perpendicular building, purchased for 10*s*. by Lady Frances Winchcombe in 1707. She presented it to a Blue Coat school which she founded in the village.

XXV

Newbury, the "hated rival," is three miles down the road. Within a mile of it in coaching times, but now not to be distinguished from the town itself, is Speenhamland, the site of that famous coaching inn, the "Pelican," whose charges were of so monumental a character that Quin has immortalized them in the lines:—

> "The famous inn at Speenhamland,
> That stands beneath the hill,
> May well be called the Pelican,
> From its enormous bill."

Alas! how are the mighty fallen! The Pelican is no longer an inn, but has been divided up, and part of it is a veterinary establishment.

RAIL AND RIVER: THE KENNET AND THE GREAT WESTERN RAILWAY.

THOMAS STACKHOUSE

The most famous inhabitant of Newbury was that fifteenth-century clothier, that "Jack of Newbury," whose wealth and public benefactions were alike considered wonderful in his day. The most notorious inhabitant was that scandalous Vicar of Beenham Vallance, near by, who flourished flamboyantly here between 1733 and 1752. Candour compels the admission that the Rev. Thomas Stackhouse, besides being the learned author of the "History of the Bible," was also a great drunkard. That history, indeed, he chiefly wrote at an inn still standing on the Bath Road near Thatcham, called "Jack's Booth." He would stay there for days at a time, and write (and drink), in an arbour in the garden, going frequently from this retreat to his church on Sundays, where, in the pulpit, he would break into incoherent prayers and maudlin tears, asking forgiveness for his besetting sin, and promising reformation of his evil courses. But after service he was generally to be seen going back to his inn. Here one day a friend found him and reminded him that it was the day of the Bishop's Visitation, a circumstance which he had quite forgotten. He went off, clothed disgracefully, and by no means sober. "Who," asked the Bishop, indignantly, on seeing this strange creature— "who is that shabby, dirty old man?" The vicar answered the query himself. "I am," he shouted, "Thomas Stackhouse, Vicar of Beenham, who wrote the 'History of the Bible,' and that is more than your lordship can do!" The historian of these things says this reply quite upset the gravity of the solemn meeting; and the statement may well be believed.

Camden says, "Newburie must acknowledge Speen as its mother," and Newbury, in fact, was originally an offshoot from Speen, which was anciently a fortified Roman settlement in the tangled underwoods of the wild country between the Roman cities of Aquæ Solis and Calleva (Bath and Silchester). The Romans called it "Spinæ," *i.e.* "the Thorns," a sufficiently descriptive title in that era. The Domesday Book calls it "Spone." The fact of Speen having been the original settlement may be partly traced in the circumstance of its lying directly on the old road, while Newbury, its infinitely bigger daughter, sprawls out on the Whitchurch and Andover roads, which run from the Bath Road almost at right angles.

There are quaint houses at Newbury, and old inns; some of them, like the "Globe" or the "King's Arms," converted into shops or private houses, while others perhaps do a brisker trade in drink than in good cheer of the more hospitable sort. There are the "White Hart," and the "Jack of Newbury," with a modern front, and others. The Kennet divides the town in half, and runs under a bridge which carries the street across its narrow width, bordered with quaint-looking houses. Here is the old Cloth Hall, a singular building, neglected now that the weaving trade has decayed; and on the west side of the bridge stands the parish church with a small brass in it to the memory of the great "Jack," and a very economical monument to a certain "J.W.C.," 1692, just roughly carved into the stonework of a buttress at the east end.

AT THE 55TH MILESTONE.

INSCRIPTION.
NEWBURY CHURCH.

It is strange to think that only twenty-seven years ago (in 1872, as a matter of fact), at Newbury, a rag and bone dealer who for several years had been well known in the town as a man of intemperate habits, and upon whom imprisonment in Reading Gaol had failed to produce any beneficial effect, was fixed in the stocks for drunkenness and disorderly conduct at Divine service in the parish church. Twenty-six years had elapsed since the stocks had last been used, and their reappearance created no little sensation and amusement, several hundreds of persons being attracted to the spot where they were fixed. The sinful rag man was seated upon a stool, and his legs were secured in the stocks at a few minutes past one. He seemed anything but pleased with the laughter and derision of the crowd. Four hours having passed, he was released.

"JACK OF NEWBURY"

It is impossible to escape Jack of Newbury in this the scene of his greatness. "John Smalwoode the elder, alias John Wynchcombe," as he describes himself in his last will and testament, in 1519, was the most prominent of the clothworkers in the reigns of the Seventh and Eighth Henrys. He is perhaps best described in the words of a pamphlet published towards the close of the sixteenth century:—"He was a man of merrie disposition and honest conversation, was wondrous well beloved of rich and poore, especially because in every place where he came he would spend his money with the best, and was not any time found a churl of his purse. Wherefore, being so good a companion, he was called of olde and younge 'Jacke of Newberie,' a man so generally well knowne in all this countrye for his good fellowship, that he could goe into no place but he found acquaintance; by means whereof Jacke could no sooner get a crowne, but straight hee found meanes to spend it; yet had he ever this care, that hee would always keepe himselfe in comely and decent apparel, neither at any time would hee be overcome in drinke, but so discreetly behave himselfe with honest mirthe and pleasant conceits, that he was every gentleman's companion."

This is so excellent a voucher for him that it is not surprising so universal a favourite stepped into the shoes of his master's widow. She was rich, and he with a plentiful lack of coin; yet though she had a choice of suitors, including a "tanner, a taylor, and a parson," she set her heart on Jack with something of the determination which characterized the "Berkshire Lady" already referred to in these pages; and though he was something loth, married him out of hand. We are not told that she regretted it, but probably she did, for the stories have it that she was a gossip and given to staying out late, while Jack stopped at home and went betimes to bed. Once, when she returned at midnight, and knocked at the door, he looked from his window and told her that, as she had stayed out all day for her own delight, she might "lie forth" until the morning for his. "Moved with pity," as the narrative says, but more likely because her continual knocking kept him awake, he at last went down in his shirt and opened the door, when "Alack, husband," says she, "what hap have I? My wedding ring was even now in my hand, and I have let it fall about the door; good, sweet John, come forth with the candle and help me seek it."

He "went forth" accordingly, into the street, and she locked him out! We are not told what happened when he got in again.

He seems to have taken her loss, a little later, calmly enough, for he speedily married again, and although "wondrous wealthie," he chose a poor girl who lived at Aylesbury. A grand wedding it was when Joan (for that was her name) and Jack were married. Her head, we are assured, was adorned with a "billement of gold, and her hair, as yellow as gold, hanging downe behind her." In fact, "Her golden hair was hanging down her back," as the music-hall songster has it; which goes far to prove that the modern *penchant* for yellow locks has a respectable antiquity, and warrants brunettes in using all the arts of the toilet to redress the errors of Nature.

JACK AS ENTERTAINER

Jack of Newbury entertained Henry the Eighth here, and, wonderful to relate, the floors of the house were covered with broad cloth, instead of the then usual rushes. Also, he equipped a hundred of his workmen, fifty as horsemen, and fifty armed with bows and pikes, "as well armed and better clothed than any," and went with them to the Scotch war. The "Ballad of the Newberrie Archers" tells us how they distinguished themselves at Flodden Field; but it must be added that it is doubtful whether they ever reached so far; which proves the ballad-maker—the "special correspondent" of that time—to have been more eloquent than truthful. That Jack was the principal man of his trade must be evident from these facts and from the statement that he employed a hundred looms; and a great deal more evident from his having been selected to head the petition of the clothiers for the encouragement of trade with France. He had a pretty taste in sarcasm, too, if his retort upon Wolsey, to whom it had been referred, and who had delayed to answer it, is considered. "If my Lord Chancellor's father," said he, "had been no hastier in killing calves than he in despatching of poor men's suits, I think he would never have worn a mitre." It is only necessary to remember that Wolsey was the son of a butcher for the sting of this quip to be appreciated.

OLD CLOTH HALL, NEWBURY.

XXVI

In 1531, and again in 1556, Newbury was the scene of martyrdoms; and in 1643 and 1644 the site of two battles between Charles and his Parliament, both almost equally indecisive, and both remarkable for desperate courage on either side.

FIRST BATTLE OF NEWBURY

The first battle was fought to the south of the town on September 18, and was the culmination of a Royalist attack upon the Parliamentary army under the Earl of Essex, on the march from Gloucester to London. Essex had designed to lie at Newbury, the town being strongly for the Parliament; but as he was marching across Enborne Chase on the 16th, his line was cut by the appearance of Prince Rupert, who charged down upon him with his dragoons. In this skirmish the Marquis de Vieuville was slain, and many others of the Royalists. The battle thus forced on by the rashness of Prince Rupert was one of the fiercest in the war.

The King was encamped near Donnington. Essex advanced and seized some elevated ground, where his men were charged by the Royalist cavalry, at whose head was the Earl of Carnarvon. Carnarvon had that morning measured a gateway with his sword, to see if it were wide enough for the prisoners who, with Essex at their head, they were to lead through it in the evening. Although they cut up Essex's cavalry, Carnarvon himself fell in that gallant charge, and was carried through the same gateway, a corpse, that night.

It was the Parliamentary foot, the London train-bands, that saved the day, which would otherwise have been a disastrous rout for their leader. They withstood the cannonading and the impetuous charges of Rupert's horse, and, with Essex himself among them, in a conspicuous white hat, drove back the Royalist infantry. It was not until night had fallen that the contest ceased. Six thousand were slain that day, and neither side had won. Essex was so weakened that he retreated upon Reading the next morning.

He had nearly reached Theale when Rupert descended upon his rear like a hurricane, and cut down many of his troops in a spot still called, from this circumstance, "Dead Man's Lane."

The Royalists perhaps had slightly the better of the First Battle of Newbury; but at what a cost! Carnarvon, the young Earl of Sunderland; and Lucius Cary, Viscount Falkland, slain! Falkland was Secretary of State, and a patriot whose feelings were above partizanship. He seems to have had a presentiment of death, for he received the Sacrament on the morning of the battle, saying, "I am weary of the times, and foresee much misery to my country; but I believe I shall be out of it ere night." There is a monument on Wash Common to him—

"The blameless and the brave,"

who fell thus with his brothers-in-arms; and mounds still mark the places where the dead were buried. The memory of this great battle has recently been revived, for in 1897 its anniversary was celebrated, and wreaths and crosses of evergreens were laid upon the monument and the tumuli.

XXVII

THE SECOND BATTLE

The Second Battle of Newbury was fought on Sunday, October 27, 1644. The thickest part of it raged round Speen, on the Bath Road, and in the gardens of Shaw House. This house, one of the finest mansions in Berkshire, was built by Thomas Dolman, clothier, in 1581. He was evidently something of a scholar, and worldly wise as well, for he knew that his riches and his grand mansion would rouse envious talk. Accordingly he caused Latin and Greek inscriptions to be carved over the entrance, which, Englished, run—

"Let no envious man enter here."

And—

"The toothless man envies the teeth of those who eat,
and the mole despises the eyes of the roe."

It is quite obvious that Thomas Dolman had been a great deal criticized locally, and that the iron of that criticism had entered his soul.

His son became Sir Thomas Dolman, and it was his descendant, Sir John Dolman, who garrisoned the house and entertained King Charles here on the night before the second battle. A hole is still shown in the panelling of the drawing-room, said to have been made by a shot fired at the King that night when standing at the window; and a brass plate records the circumstance in a Latin inscription.

THE LAST OF THE SMOCK-FROCKS AND BEAVERS.

The parapets of Shaw House were lined with Royalist musketeers on this occasion, and entrenchments thrown up in the gardens; but after a stubbornly contested fight the Royalists were too weakened to retain the position. Their ordnance and the wounded were left at Donnington Castle, a mile away, and they fell back upon Oxford. Neither side had been sorry when night fell and put an end to a hard-fought, but inconclusive, day; and for their part the Parliamentary leaders were glad to see the King's forces withdrawing by the light of the moon, and did not dare risk an attack upon them.

It is not a little singular that during all this clash of arms the Royalist governor of Donnington Castle held that stronghold, although repeatedly attacked, from August, 1644, to April, 1646, and then only surrendered when desired by the King to do so.

CURIOUS OLD TOLL-HOUSE BETWEEN NEWBURY AND HUNGERFORD.

SPEEN

The road ascends to Speen, or, as it is often called, "Church Speen." The present writer was climbing it when he overtook a countryman in a smock-frock, to whom the steep gradient was evidently anything but welcome.

"You're a regular Mountjoy, a' b'lieve," said the countryman, puffing and blowing.

"A regular what?"

"A Mountjoy—a walker. But there; you bain't Newbury?"

I told him I certainly was not a native of that town.

"Well," said he, "you won't, never have heerd of 'un, p'raps."

It seems, then, that about fifty years ago Newbury boasted a pedestrian of that name, who obtained such a great local reputation that he has become proverbial with the country people, so that a "regular Mountjoy" is any one who possesses good walking powers.

Church Speen passed, an undulating road leads past a curiously castellated old toll-house to Hungerford.

XXVIII

It is at Hungerford, sixty-four miles from Hyde Park Corner, that one leaves Berkshire and enters Wilts, coming into wilder and less pastoral country. Hungerford town, however, is just within the Berkshire borders. The constant Kennet flows across the road here, and is crossed by a substantial bridge, from whose parapets anglers may be seen patiently waiting to lure the wily trout from their swims. Fuller quaintly says: "Good and great trouts are found in the river of Kennet nigh Hungerford; they are in their perfection in the month of May, and yearly decline with the buck. Being come to his full growth, he decays in goodness, not greatness, and thrives in his head till his death. Note, by the way, that an hog-back and little head is a sign that any fish is in season."

The chief street of Hungerford lies along the road to Salisbury, and the cyclist who is intent upon "doing" the Bath Road without turning to thoroughly explore the places along its course, consequently sees little of the town beyond the few old mansions and cottages, and the old coaching inn, "The Bear," which front the highway. Not much, however, is in this case lost, for Hungerford contains little of interest, and were it not for its singular Hocktide customs, and for the fact that it was the first town to obtain the free delivery of letters between its post-office and the houses to which letters were addressed, would scarce demand an extended notice.

OLD POST-OFFICE CUSTOMS

The original plan of the General Post-Office, all over the country, was to allow postmasters of country towns to demand a fee for delivery. Those who expected letters were supposed to call for them. If they desired them to be delivered, the additional fee was a penny or twopence, according to the conscience or the cupidity of the postmaster, whose perquisites these fees were. This applied to houses quite near post-offices, and even next door to them. This extraordinary state of affairs was borne with for some time, until at last several towns brought actions against the Post-Office to decide if prepaid postage ought not to ensure delivery in the boundaries of post-towns. Hungerford was selected by the Courts as a typical case, and secured a judgment in its favour, Michaelmas, 1774.

Hocktide is a stirring time in this little town of less than three thousand inhabitants. It is determined by Eastertide, and generally falls in April. The odd observances derive their origin from the conditions imposed by John of Gaunt, father of Henry the Fourth, who, in the fourteenth century, conferred the rights and privileges of common-land and fishing in the Kennet upon the town. To hand down the proof of his gift to posterity, he presented with the charter a brass horn which bears the inscription:—

> "John a Gaun did giue and
> grant the Riall of Fishing to
> Hungerford Toune from Eldren
> Stub to Irish stil excepting som
> Seueral mil Pound
> Jehosphat Lucas was Cunstabl."

Not this horn, but its seventeenth-century successor, is jealously preserved in the Town Hall. It has a capacity of one quart.

HOCK TIDE

As an unreformed borough, Hungerford still enjoys the old-time custom of appointing, in the place of Mayor and Corporation, a Constable, Portreeve, Bailiff, Tithing-men, Keeper of the Keys of the Coffers, Hayward, Water Bailiffs, Ale-tasters, and Bellman. The ceremonies begin on the Friday before Hock Tuesday with a "macaroni supper and punchbowl," and are held at the "John of Gaunt" inn. Tuesday, however, is the great day, when at an early hour the bellman goes round the borough commanding all those who hold land or dwellings within the confines of the town to appear at the Hockney, under pain of a poll-tax of one penny, called the "head-penny." Lest this warning should be insufficient, he mounts to the balcony of the Town Hall, where he blows a blast upon the horn. Those who do not obey the summons and refuse the payment of the head-penny are liable to lose their rights to the privileges of the borough.

HUNGERFORD.

By nine o'clock the jury are assembled in the Town Hall for the transaction of their annual business, and immediately after they are sworn in, the two tithing-men start on their round of the town. It is in this part of the proceedings that most interest is taken, for the business of the tithing-men is to take a poll-tax of twopence from every male inhabitant and a kiss from the wives and daughters of the burgesses. This is in recognition of the ancient powers of the Lord of the Manor, who had peculiar rights over the property and persons of his "chattels," as the people were once regarded.

HUNGERFORD TUTTI-MEN.

The tithing-men are known as tutti-men; tutti being the local word for pretty. They carry short poles as insignia of office, gaily bedecked with blue ribbons and choice flowers known as tutti-poles; while behind them walks a man groaning under the weight of the tutti oranges, it being the custom to bestow an orange upon every person who is kissed, as well as upon the school and workhouse children. The rights of office having been duly vested in them by means of strange customs and exhortation, the two favoured ones start off down the High Street on their kissing mission, followed by the orange-bearer and greeted with the cheers of the assembled people. One by one the houses are entered, and the custom observed both in spirit and letter; nor is it confined to the young and comely, for the old dames of Hungerford would deem themselves, if not insulted, at least sadly neglected, were the tutti-men to pass their houses unentered. Usually these officers find little difficulty in carrying out their pleasant duties, but sometimes the excitement is increased by some coy maiden, whose rustic simplicity prompts her to run away or hide. But as a general rule the ladies of Hungerford show very little objection to the observance of the ancient customs, so that the labours of the tutti-men are considerably lightened.

Thus, amid laughter, merriment, and mock-seriousness, the fun is continued until about half the borough is visited, by which time the tutti-men have taken care that all the duty kisses that should gratify the ancient inhabitants have been administered, as well as certain others that are more a pleasure than a duty. Certainly they deserve well of the town, for the tutti-men go through a good day's work by the time dinner is served. Then, in accordance with the time-honoured precedent, the Chief Constable is elected into the chair; the great bowl of punch is placed on the table after dinner, and the various offices toasted and replied for. One is drunk in solemn silence—that of John of Gaunt, the town's benefactor. All the townspeople seem satisfied with their day's carnival, save, perhaps, a crooning old burgher, who may occasionally be heard to extol the good old days when the punch was strong and the newly-elected officers went home in wheelbarrows.

XXIX

LITTLECOTE

From the everyday respectable dulness of Hungerford itself we will pass to the exciting scandals which make up much of the story of Littlecote, that gloomy and romantic Tudor mansion, which has become famous (or infamous, if you will have it so) through the crimes and debaucheries of Will Darell. There are two ways of reaching Littlecote from the Bath Road. The most obvious way is by turning to the right when in the midst of Hungerford town; the other, which is the more rural, is by a lane a mile further down the road. Either will bring the traveller to that secluded spot in the course of three and a half miles.

It stands, that hoary pile, in a wide and well-wooded park, sheltered beneath the swelling Wiltshire downs and close beside the gentle Kennet, whose stream has been fruitful of trout ever since "trouts" (as our ancestors quaintly called them, in the plural) were angled for. Littlecote, as we now see it, was built by the Darells in the closing years of the fifteenth century, in whose early years it had passed from the Colston family by the marriage of the heiress of the Colstons to William Darell, son of Sir William Darell, of Sesay, in Yorkshire. A descendant of this emigrant from the North Riding, the "Wild Will Darell" of this blood-boltered history was born into an estate comprising an ancestral home and many thousands of acres in the counties of Wilts, Berks, and Hants, and might have been accounted fortunate had it not been for the rather more than trifling circumstances of an unhappy upbringing which included a shameful treatment of himself and his mother by an unnatural father; the paternal extravagances which had alienated much of the property; the heavy charge made on the estate for the benefit of the mistress of his brother, who preceded him in the estate; and, finally, the crop of lawsuits into which he was plunged immediately upon succeeding to this singularly-encumbered patrimony. At this interval of time it has become quite impossible for serious historians to discriminate between the facts and the—fancies, shall we call them?—of the Wild Darell story. This difficulty does not arise from lack of patient research on the part of Darell commentators, who have ransacked the Record Office to prove that he was *not* a villain of the most lurid kind, or the industry of others who have searched among musty muniment chests to determine that he *was*. It would, considering the fact of the records in the Littlecote muniment room not having yet been explored for the benefit of these historic doubts, be rash indeed for any one to pronounce definitely for either of the very diverse views held of Darell as Villain, or Darell as Good Young Man.

The story, which first became widely known through a footnote appended to Sir Walter Scott's "Rokeby," is of a midwife summoned from the village of Shefford, seven miles away, on a false pretence of attending Lady Knyvett, of Charlton, near by, and of her being blindfolded and led on horseback in the darkness of the night to quite another house, in one of whose stately rooms lay a mysterious masked lady for whom her services were required. The horrid legend then goes on to say that a tall, slender gentleman, a lowering and ferocious-looking man, "havinge uppon hym a goune of blacke velvett," entered the room with some others, and, without a word, took the child from her arms and threw it upon a blazing fire in an ante-room, crushing it into the flaming logs with his boot-heel, so that it was presently consumed.

A prime horror, this, and rich in ferocity, mystery, and all the incertitude that comes of age and conflicting testimony. Masked lady, blindfolded nurse, burnt baby, taciturn and horrible stranger, what lurid figures are these! and how royally abused for the possession of an over-imaginative mind would be that novelist who should dare conceive incidents so romantic!

WILD DARELL

Scott gleaned his traditions from the weird legends current in the countryside. They had, when he first printed them, been the fireside gossip of that district for over two hundred years, and of course in that length of time had lost nothing in the repetition. For that reason we are asked nowadays to discredit them altogether. We cannot, however, do that, because there came to light some years ago the actual deposition to the facts made by the midwife, Mrs. Barnes of Shefford, taken down on her deathbed by a Mr. Bridges of Great Shefford, a magistrate, who was also a cousin of Darell, and would not, it may well be supposed, be inclined to spread any baseless gossip to the hurt of a family with which he was connected. This deposition tells the story as already narrated. It does not identify Darell or Littlecote, nor does it even hint the identity of *any* person or place. But the sinister discovery, some twenty years ago, at Longleat, of an original letter from Sir H. Knyvett, of Charlton, to Sir John Thynne, of Longleat, dated January 2, 1578/9 (about the time of the midwife's confession), brings us to the original rumours pointing to Darell's being the man and Littlecote the place.

LITTLECOTE.

DEATH OF DARELL

There was then residing at Longleat a Mr. Bonham, whose sister was well known to be living with Darell as his mistress, and this letter requests that "Mr. Bonham will inquire of his sister touching her usage at Will. Darell's, the birth of her children, how many there were, and what became of them: for that the report of the murder of one of them was increasing foully, and would touch Will. Darell to the quick." To that letter there is no reply, and it remains uncertain whether Darell was ever arraigned for murder and acquitted (as the story goes), or whether the rumours simply were never crystallized into a definite charge against him. The probability seems to be that he never was called upon to stand his trial. It is quite certain, however, that the legend of his being haunted along the roads by the apparition of a burning infant which startled his horse so that Wild Darell was thrown and killed is a more or less pleasing invention. Darell died quite peacefully in his bed, at Littlecote, eleven years after the midwife's death, and was buried in the Darell Chapel at Ramsbury, where he was laid to rest, October 1st, 1589. Notwithstanding these well-ascertained facts, Darell is now, if we are to credit the stories of the country-side, an apparition himself, and superstitious rustics still fear to face the roads o' nights because of a Burning Babe and a Spectral Horseman, who comes dashing down them at a terror-stricken gallop, mounted on a horse of coal-black hue, with a breath like steam and eyes like burning coals!

As for the elaborate embroideries added to the Wild Darell story from time to time, there are many. According to these ingenious fictions, the midwife counted the stairs of the strange house, and cut a piece out of the bed curtains, which she carried away. By these means; by finding the number of the stairs at Littlecote to tally with her counting, and by fitting her piece of tapestry to a hole in the curtains of a bed at Littlecote, we are told to believe the truth of the story. The singular thing, however, is that Mrs. Barnes made absolutely no mention of these things in her deposition. There remains, it is true, the fact already alluded to, that the magistrate who took down the woman's statement was a connection of Darell's, and might possibly have suppressed facts which could point to his relative being concerned in the affair. Another story is that upon Darell being arraigned (which in itself is uncertain), he made interest with Sir John Popham, the Chief Justice, to procure an acquittal.

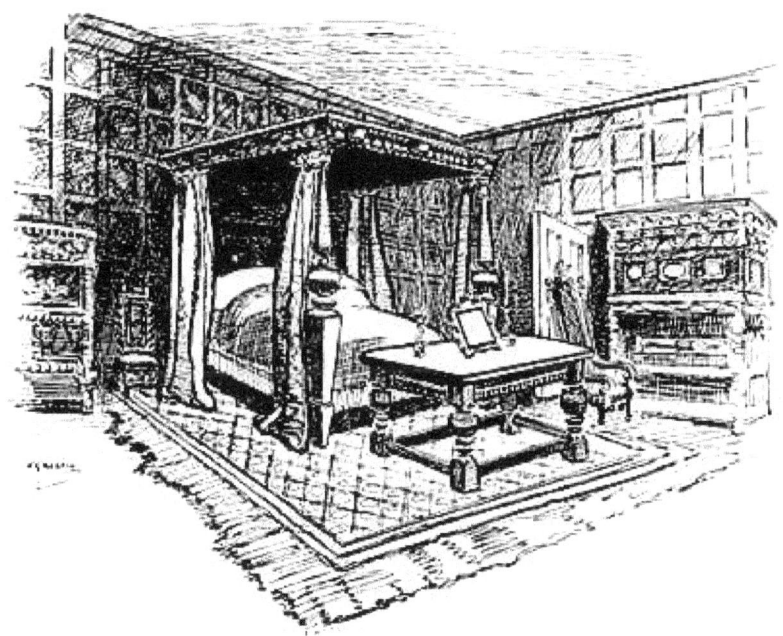

THE HAUNTED CHAMBER.

Now it is quite certain that Popham did not become Chief Justice until 1592, when Darell had been in his grave nearly three years, and could not therefore have done so. He was, it is true, Attorney-General at the time of Darell's supposed crime, and, *had* there been a trial, and *had* he been bribed, could possibly have procured a *nolle prosequi*.

But Darell certainly made over the reversion of Littlecote to Popham in 1586, and Popham took possession upon Darell's decease. The story of this transaction being the bribe in question we owe to Aubrey, the county historian (or rather, the county gossip), who actually gives an account of the trial and says, "Sir John Popham gave sentence according to law, but being a great person and a favourite, he pronounced a *noli prosequi*."

More to the point is the fact that Darell, in 1583, offered Lord Chancellor Bromley the then large sum of £5000 to be "his good friend."

Those who are interested in the Darell story are equally divided as to his general character. One would have us believe that he was a Model Squire, who fished for trout, took an enthralling interest in his flower-garden, and if he did not always come home to tea (because tea not having at that period been introduced, it was impossible to do so), was content with a modest pint of claret at dinner, and spent the rest of the evening in reading what improving literature was to be had in the Elizabethan age; which, I fear, judging from the general character of the time, was of a somewhat meagre nature.

THE REAL DARELL

The real Darell was not quite like that picture. We already know that he had one mistress at Littlecote, and then there was Lady Anne Hungerford, an elderly charmer, whom by some means Wild Will had seduced from her husband, and whose letters, still preserved, to her "deare Dorrell" are not so improving as the recipient's other reading. One learns from these choice communications that Lady Anne had been accused of murder, adultery, and trying to poison her husband; and, under the circumstances, it seems quite likely that all these charges were well-founded, even though she says that "luker and gaine makes many dissembling and hollow hearts" (which sounds like one of the admirable copy-book maxims of our youth), and that she anticipates being cleared from suspicion of these "vill and abomynabell practiscis." Add to these hot-blooded intrigues the extravagances which, together with his litigious disposition, served to ruin his estate and to bring him into disfavour with his neighbours, and we obtain the genesis of all the ill-favoured legends of this picturesque figure of the Elizabethan era.

XXX

THE GREAT REBELLION

Littlecote had not done with stirring scenes when Darell was dead and the Pophams took possession. The Great Hall, hung round with pikes, leather jerkins, helmets, and cuirasses of Cromwellian times, serves to tell, in its warlike array, of how the place became a rendezvous of the Roundheads of this vicinity. These relics are the arms and accoutrements of the Popham Horse, raised by Colonel Alexander Popham, whose own suit of armour is still suspended here, over one of the doorways. A fitting place this, then, for that gathering of the King's Commissioners who came to Littlecote in December, 1688. The occasion was an historic one. James the Second was tottering upon his throne, and the Prince of Orange, invited to these shores to protect the civil and religious liberties of the nation, had marched up with his Dutchmen from his landing in the West Country. No man knew what would be the course of events, because not one of those concerned in that memorable crisis knew his own mind, from the King and his adherents on the one side, to the Prince and his partisans on the other.

The two parties met at Hungerford on December 8. On the following day, Sunday, the Commissioners dined at Littlecote, and then and there the fate of the kingdom was settled, quite amicably. The old Hall was crowded with Peers and Generals—Halifax, the judicious "trimmer," whose cautious diplomacy guided the crisis through to its solution without bloodshed; Burnet, Nottingham, Shrewsbury, and Oxford, all waiting upon events. Halifax, the partisan of the King, seized the opportunity of extracting from Burnet all he knew and thought. "Do you wish to get the King into your power?" he asked the Bishop. "Not at all," replied Burnet: "we would not do the least harm to his person." "And if he were to go away?" slyly insinuated Halifax. "There is nothing so much to be wished," whispered the Bishop, apprehending his meaning; and so James slunk away, and William of Orange reigned in his stead.

For the rest, Littlecote is a veritable storehouse of art and antiquities. The collection of ancient armour in the Great Hall is one of the finest in England. Here, too, is Chief Justice Popham's chair, and the thumbstocks which he used as a means of extracting confessions from petty offenders with whom persuasion of the merely moral kind had failed. Then there is the painting of Mr. Popham's horse, "Wild Dayrell," which won the Derby in 1855, and many interesting objects besides. First in point of interest, however, is the Haunted Chamber, which is even now said to resound with groans and imprecations; and is still very much in the same condition as in Darell's day, although, to be sure, the fateful ante-room is now divided from it. Darell's

Tree, an ancient elm, patched and chained together, is still to be seen on the south side of the house, carefully tended; the legend running that Littlecote will flourish so long as its hoary trunk holds together.

XXXI

But to return to the road, which presently comes to the charming village of Froxfield, with its wide village green and great red-brick barracks of almshouses, founded in 1686 by Sarah, Duchess of Somerset, for fifty clergymen's widows, and perched up on a bank above the right-hand side of the highway.

SAVERNAKE FOREST

Thence, nearly all the way into Marlborough, seven miles ahead, the road lies through Savernake Forest and its outskirts, passing the loveliest forest scenery in England. Nothing can compare for magnificence with the massed beeches and oaks of Savernake, whose glorious alleys of foliage extend for miles in every direction. These fine full-grown trees are planted for the most part in a well-considered design, and radiate from a central point in eight directions. These "Eight Walks," as they are called, vary in length from four miles downwards, and lie to the south of the road. The highway runs through the northern verge of the Forest, quite open and hedgeless all the way, with two gates across it, about two miles apart. The scenery is like nothing so much as a painting by De Wint or Constable.

The Marquis of Ailesbury, to whom this noble demesne (the only Forest in the possession of a subject) belongs, has his residence near the southern boundary of the Forest, at Tottenham House, which is a singularly plain building externally, and so reminiscent in name of the Tottenham Court Road that it would have been exquisitely appropriate had the late Marquis sold the estate to Sir John Blundell Maple instead of to Lord Iveagh.

I suppose the eccentricities of the late Marquis of Ailesbury will become the subject of curious legends in the coming by-and-by. He was born out of his time, and was a kind of "throw-back" to earlier types that flourished when the Prince Regent and the Toms and Jerrys disported themselves in the famous Corinthian manner.

The glades of Savernake still remain in the family, but were alienated to Lord Iveagh, the man of Dublin stout, of whom the quaint Biblical conceit was invented by some temperance wag: "He who is not for us is agin us.[3] He brews XX." Lord Iveagh bought the estates and paid for them, but the House of Lords refused to sanction the sale, and so Savernake still belongs to the Brudenell-Bruces.

The late Marquis had a perfect genius for dissipating wealth. A "horsey" man among the "horsey," his favourite companions were sporting men of the more unrefined type, and he was hail-fellow with the cab-men and 'bus-men of London. Radicals found in his career a text for their discourses and a reason for abolishing the House of Lords as an hereditary chamber; and the ballet-girls of the London theatres regarded him as all a Peer should be. One who knew "Lord Stomach-ache," as he was playfully nicknamed before he had succeeded to the Marquisate and was yet Lord Savernake, said—

"The wealth and colour of his lordship's language surprised me. I never knew or heard a costermonger in the Dials with such a repertory. I saw him once with a couple of choice friends on a costermonger's barrow, such as is used for hawking fish or vegetables. One 'pal' had a 'yard of tin' (or coaching horn), on which he tootled melodiously. His lordship wore a very high collar, a blue birds-eye belcher fastened with a nursery-pin for a necktie, a huge drab box-cloth coat with large mother-o'-pearl buttons, a low-crowned, broad-brimmed coachman's hat, and a very tight pair of trousers. It was raining, a pitiless, pelting drizzle, and as they pulled up for drinks, he took off his heavy coat, and, placing it carefully over the patient 'moke,' said to it, as he patted it, 'There y'are, Neddy; that'll keep the bloomin' wet off you, old bloke, won't it?'"

For my own part, I think the latter part of that incident is the most creditable thing on record in the "short and merry" life of poor "Stomach-ache."

OLD TIMES ON THE ROAD

Savernake Forest left behind, the road descends steeply down Forest Hill in the direction of Marlborough. This hill was one of the worst obstacles met with between London and Bath in the old times, and its steepness was then rendered more difficult by reason of the execrable surface of the road. This is the experience of one travelling to London about 1816: "Twenty times at least the eight horses came to a standstill, and had to be allowed their own time before they would move. For more than half the way up there lay an extensive encampment of gipsies along each side of the road, forming a most picturesque scene with their wild figures, their bright-coloured costumes, and dark bronzed skin; their white tents, and the numerous columns of blue, thin smoke that curled upwards and lost itself in the dense foliage. These stout vagabonds rendered us an essential service; they cheered and lashed the horses, they pushed bodily in the rear, and they climbed the spokes of the revolving wheels, to send them round, with a recklessness and dexterity only acquired by long practice. To compensate them for their labour, the coachman halted at the top of the hill to give them a chance of trading; and then the women came forward and did a little fortune-telling with the ladies, not without joking and bantering on the part of the onlookers; while the younger gipsies brought abundance of sweet wood-strawberries, dished up in dock-leaves, than which nothing at the time could have been more welcome.

"During the first half of the journey to London our pace would not average more than four miles an hour, and sometimes the tramps and wanderers of the road would keep up with us for the hour together, especially the pedlars and packmen, who would display their Brummagem wares, and now and then effect a sale as we rumbled along."

A wide view extends from here, over the valley of the Kennet, with Marlborough lying in its hollow, and the Wiltshire downs, stretching away in bare rolling masses, in the direction of Swindon. Marlborough develops itself slowly as one descends, and becomes lost for a time as the panoramic view sinks out of sight.

XXXII

MARLBOROUGH

There are fine old inns at Marlborough; coaching inns, fallen from the high estate that was theirs in the days when Pepys and Sheridan, my Lord Chatham with his gout and his innumerable train of servants, and Horace Walpole with his gimcrackery and his caustic comments upon the kind of society in which he found himself upon the Bath Road, stayed here. No one comes here nowadays with vast retinues of lackeys, and the man does not exist, be he Peer or Commoner, who could dare be so offensive as that haughty and insufferable personage, the aforesaid Earl of Chatham, who, nursing his gout at the "Castle" Hotel in 1762, practically converted the place to his own exclusive use, regardless of the comfort or convenience of any one else. He would not stay at the "Castle," he said, storming at the terrified landlord, unless all the servants of the establishment were forthwith clothed in the Chatham livery. And so clothed they were, and the "Castle" became for some weeks what it had been before the strange workings of fate had converted it into the finest of all the inns along the road to Bath—the private residence of a nobleman.

There are breakneck streets in Marlborough, for the town, although built in the valley, has the entrance to its principal street carried round the spur of a foothill so that one side of the thoroughfare is considerably lower than the other, and the humorous among Marlborough's neighbours declare that bicycles are the only vehicles that can be driven round by the Town Hall without upsetting. But, in spite of what Cobbett says in his "Rural Rides," that "Marlborough is an ill-looking place enough," this street is the finest, broadest, neatest, and most picturesque of any along these hundred odd miles of highway. Think of all the adjectives that make for admiration, and you have scarce employed one that overrates the dignified and stately air of the High Street of Marlborough. The width of the road is accounted for by its having been used as a market-place; the architectural character of the houses lining it is due to the fires that devastated the town in 1653, 1679, and 1690, burning down the older houses, and causing the town to be almost wholly rebuilt. Those were the days of the Renaissance, and before the dwelling-house became frankly unornamental and merely a brick or stone box for people to live in, with window and door holes from which they could look or issue forth.

Thanks, then, to these fires, Marlborough is to-day a town of architectural delights, while the older portion of the College is fully as interesting, having been built on the site of the old Castle from designs by Inigo Jones or his son-in-law, Webb. It is thus a noble view along the High Street: the shops, which are interspersed among the private houses, being here and there fronted with covered ways, forming dry walks in wet weather; an arcaded Market House and Town Hall at the eastern end, and a church closing the view in each direction.

MARLBOROUGH.

ARCADIAN HUMBUG

Marlborough College is at the western end of this street, occupying the fine mansion built by Francis, Lord Seymour, in time to entertain Charles the Second, who with his Queen, his brother, and a crowded suite halted here on his way to the West, in one of his Royal progresses. It became the residence of that Earl of Hertford whose Countess had a gushing affection for those tame poets of the eighteenth century whose blank verse was so soothing to the senses and so absolutely restful to the mind—requiring little mental exercise to write, and none at all to read. My Lady held quite a poetic court, of which Pope, Dr. Watts, and Thomson were the shining lights, and squirted amiable piffle about Chloes and Strephons while her fine London guests strutted about the emerald lawns pretending to be Wiltshire peasantry; the ladies wielding shepherds' crooks, and leading lambs made presentable with much expenditure of soap and water, in leashes of sky-blue silk; while the gallant gentlemen, more used, we may be sure, to dining and drinking, learned to play upon oaten reeds, and were quite idyllic and Arcadian. What an astounding time! and how disgusted these fine folks would have been, had they been forced to fare on the fat bacon and small beer of the real shepherds, instead of the kickshaws and the port which helped them to sustain their affectations! The spectacle of that vicious era, pretending to rural simplicity is, perhaps, the most notable example of vice paying homage to virtue that may be given. The folly of the age is almost inconceivable, but it is all preserved for us and duly certified in its literature and in the pictures of the school of Watteau; while this particular instance of it may be voluminously read of in the records of the time, or be conjured up by a sight of the winding walks and grottoes in the Castle gardens, where, perhaps, Dr. Watts may have seen the original busy bee that gave him the first notion of—

> "How doth the little busy bee
> Employ each shining hour,
> By gath'ring honey all the day
> From ev'ry opening flower."

Meanwhile, Thomson was sipping nectar (which is Greek for brandy-punch) with my Lord Hertford, and babbling of other things than green fields. In fact, the literary Lady Hertford found the poet of the "Seasons" to be a drunkard, and he was not invited to any more of her parties.

The house passed at length to the Dukes of Northumberland, who neglected it, and at last leased it to a Mr. Cotterell, an innkeeper, who with prophetic vision saw custom coming down the road in an increasing tide. Appropriately known as the "Castle," it remained an hotel until January 5, 1843, when its doors were finally closed, to be re-opened as the home of the newly established "Marlborough College."

For nearly a century the "Castle" entertained the best society in the land. Forty-two coaches passed through the town every day when it was at the height of its prosperity, and a goodly proportion of their occupants stayed here. Take, in fact, the lists of distinguished arrivals at Bath during that time, and you have practically a visitors' list of the "Castle."

Marlborough College was established in this house of entertainment, and new buildings have been added from time to time; but the old "Castle Hotel" may yet be traced from its characteristic architecture. Amid its pleasant lawns and gardens rises that prehistoric hill on which Marlborough Castle was built. Indeed, here, in this "Castle Mound," is the very fount and origin of the town, whose very name is supposed to derive from this earthwork, being the grave of the magician Merlin, who with his enchantments is said to lie here still, until Britain shall be in need of him again. "Merleberg," or "Merlin's town," is said to have been Marlborough's first name, and the crest over the town arms still represents the Mound, with a motto in Latin to "the bones of the wise Merlin."[4]

XXXIII

THE KENNET

When the traveller leaves Marlborough he bids good-bye, for many miles yet to come, to the pleasant forest groves, the rich, low-lying pastures, and the fishful streams that have bordered the road hitherto. The valley of the Kennet is, it is true, near by, and for the next six miles it may be glimpsed, on the left, like some Promised Land of Plenty; but the road itself is bare. The "green pastures and still waters" of the Psalmist, indeed, you think when mounting gradually out of Marlborough you see the pleasant water-meadows afar off as you toil up the shoulder of the downs, passing a picturesque roadside inn, the "Marquis of Ailesbury's Arms," and the village of Fyfield on the way, with a glimpse of Manton village down below, amid its elms and farmyards by the windings of the stream.

ROADSIDE INN, MANTON.

Fyfield (how many dozens of Fyfields are there in England?) is tiny, clean, and quaint, with a pinnacled church tower on to whose roof you look down from the road, and may glimpse in a backward glance the whole of the district traversed since Savernake Forest was left behind. There, in long dark clumps upon the distant hilly horizon are the grand avenues of that forest; the Bath Road descending from them like a white ribbon into Marlborough town, whose houses are hid, only the church towers shining white in the sun, against a green background. Ahead rises unenclosed downland, with chalky, flint-strewn road, the unenclosed wastes of green-grey grass, broken here and there with mounds, grass-grown too.

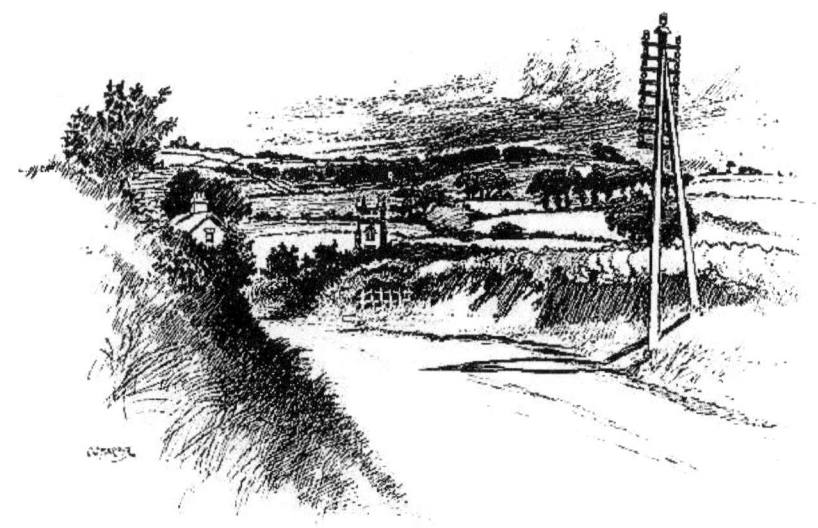

FYFIELD.

MARLBOROUGH DOWNS

On the left hand, at the distance of half a mile, perhaps, rises the church of West Overton, an offence here in its newness, for this road is Roman, these mounds are ancient British graves, and everywhere, look in what direction you will on these bleak and treeless wastes, are the mysterious vestiges of a people who had no arts, no science, no literature, who lived, in fact, a savage nomadic life, but who, for all those disabilities, have left records of their passing that may well remain when the civilization of to-day has perished. On these downs are countless tumuli; in the hollows are unnumbered thousands of stones, brought no one knows whence, or for what purpose, and the remains of cromlechs may be seen that add to the complex puzzle of the wherefore of it all. West Kennet village stands in the succeeding hollow, like some shamed modern trespasser, amid these prehistoric remains which appear, Sphinx-like, on the sky-line or stand lonely in the folds of the barren hills.

The district seems to have been a metropolis of the prehistoric dead (if, indeed, all these ruined stone avenues and circles are sepulchral), or some vast open-air cathedral of a forgotten faith; if they have a religious rather than a mortuary significance. For, but little over a mile distant, are the remains of the so-called "Druid Temple" at Avebury, a monument second only to Stonehenge in mystery, and a good deal more impressive in appearance; while, frowning down upon the highway, and standing immediately beside it, is that "greatest earthwork in Europe," Silbury Hill.

Avebury village stands on the road to Swindon, on the borders of Marlborough Downs, and has been built within a great circle which appears to have been approached by an avenue of standing stones. A few of these may still be observed, standing beside the hedgeless road. Some idea of the vast size and impressive aspect of this circular monument of those dim ages before history began may be obtained when it is said that it consists of an excavation 40 feet deep and 4442 feet in circumference, encircled on the outer side with an earthwork 40 feet high, the whole enclosing nearly 29 acres. On the inner brink of this deep fosse there are now left thirty-five huge stones out of the original number of about one thousand. Nine of these are upright, ten thrown down, and sixteen buried. Traces of pits show where the farmers of many years ago dug up the others and took them away for building-stones or gateposts. Over six hundred and fifty others are known to have been destroyed, the cottages of Avebury and the roads having been built of their fragments. How the unknown builders of this weird place could have brought these huge rocks, some of them measuring fourteen feet in length, and all weighing many tons a-piece, from unguessed distances, remains a mystery.

MARLBOROUGH DOWNS, NEAR WEST OVERTON.

AVEBURY

The first mention of Avebury Temple is by Aubrey the antiquary. It was in 1648 that he first saw the place, which seems, curiously enough, to have been until then quite unknown. He came upon it quite by chance, when hunting, and must have been astonished at the discovery of so extraordinary a place. His account of it led that kingly amateur of science, Charles the Second, to visit Avebury on his way to Bath in 1668. Pepys, too, going to Bath, unexpectedly happened both upon Avebury and Silbury Hill, and viewed them and the sepulchral barrows that, crowned with pine trees, look down from the hill sides, with an admiration not unmixed with a superstitious dread.

AVEBURY.

The road to Swindon goes straight through this great earthwork, and is crossed midway by another; together, with part of the village built within the circle, cutting it up lamentably.

SILBURY HILL.

SILBURY HILL

Silbury Hill, which stands within sight, is a fitting pendant to these mysteries. Antiquaries have contended together in referring both to ancient Britons, Phœnicians, Danes, Saxons, and even Romans, and are divided in opinion as to their object: whether they were intended for Druids' or Snake-worshippers' temples, or whether they marked the last resting-places of those slain in some great battle fought before the dawn of history. That Silbury Hill stood here when the Romans came seems, however, to be certain from the fact that the old Roman road from *Cunetio* to *Aquæ Solis* (the existing Bath Road between Marlborough and Bath), engineered along the whole of its course in a perfectly straight line, swerves slightly from the south base of the hill, evidently to avoid injuring it. A learned antiquary (but the most learned must be reduced to the level of the most ignorant before these mute earthworks) considers that Silbury was raised to commemorate a battle, probably Arthur's second and last battle of Badon Hill. The same authority thinks Avebury to be a burying-place of the dead slain in a great battle, and planned to show the dispositions of the forces engaged on either side.

But Silbury remains inscrutable. It is wholly an artificial hill, somewhat pyramidical in shape, and 170 feet in height. Its base covers five acres of ground, and was once surrounded by a stone circle, of which scanty traces are now left. The contents of it are estimated at 468,170 cubic yards of earth. Repeated attempts have been made to pluck out the heart of this mystery, but without success. So far back as 1777 it was mined from above by a party of Cornish miners, who worked under the direction of the then Duke of Northumberland and others, but nothing was discovered. Then in 1849 it was tunnelled from the base to the centre, where a space of twelve feet in diameter was examined, with the same disappointing result. Antiquaries consequently regard Silbury with hungry and expectant eyes.

Just beyond this baffling relic stands the Beckhampton inn, where the "coaches dined" and changed teams, and where the Bath Road divides into the two routes; the right-hand road going through Calne, Chippenham, and Box; the other reaching Bath by way of Devizes and Melksham. Some coaches went one way and some the other. The crack coaches, including the "Beaufort Hunt," went by the former, which is two and a half miles shorter, and is the classic route, and always the one selected nowadays by record-breaking cyclists.

XXXIV

The road between Newbury and Bath was in coaching days known as the "lower ground." So far as physical geography goes, however, the land is a great deal higher, and much more hilly than the "upper ground" between London and Newbury, and it is not to be wondered at that accidents would sometimes happen here. This, then, was the scene of an accident to a coach driven by a gay young blade, one "Jack Everett;" an accident in which he and an elderly lady passenger had a broken leg each. Both sufferers were put into a cart filled with straw, and taken to the nearest surgeon. On the road into Marlborough the coachman beguiled the tedium of the way and the pain of his injured limb by saying to the old lady, "I have often kissed a young woman, and I don't see why I shouldn't kiss an old one"—and he suited the action to the words.

THE CHERHILL WHITE HORSE

Beckhampton inn, whose real sign is the "Waggon and Horses," is the place mentioned by Dickens in the "Bagman's Story" in the *Pickwick Papers*. It remains as old-fashioned to-day as ever,[5] but does not very closely resemble the word-picture Dickens draws of it. He probably made acquaintance with the downs and the inn only in passing on his way between Bath and London in 1835. It stands at a spot where the road promises to become more cheerful and less gaunt and inhospitable; but the promise is not kept, the way going inexorably again along downs as bare as before, for another two miles. All the way between here and Cherhill village the "Lansdowne Column" is seen crowning the rolling hills to the left front. Built within the ramparts of an ancient hill-fort of the Danes, who encamped naturally enough in the most inaccessible position they could find, this "column," which is an obelisk, is an exceedingly prominent object in every direction. As one proceeds and turns the flank of the hill, the strange sight of a trotting White Horse is seen carved in the chalk of its swelling shoulder. This is not one of the ancient White Horses that decorate the hillsides of some parts of the West County and date from Anglo-Saxon times, but dates only from 1780, when it was cut by Dr. Allsop, an eccentric physician of Calne. The site it occupies is said to be the highest point between London and Bath, and the White Horse is supposed to be visible for thirty miles—which there is no occasion to believe. The figure measures 157 feet from head to tail, and the eye alone is 12 feet in diameter. The way the figure was designed is just a little curious.

No one could possibly have correctly traced the outlines of so huge an affair, except by external aid, which probably accounts for the bad drawing of the ancient examples. Dr. Allsop adopted the plan of stationing himself on the downs in full view of the rough draft, so to speak, which he had already staked out with flags, and of shouting directions to his workmen by the aid of a speaking-trumpet.

The hillside is so steep at this point that when the White Horse was restored in 1876, a workman was nearly killed by a truck load of chalk descending upon him down the slope.

Passing this interesting spot and the village of Cherhill, which lies hidden to the right of the road, the highway reaches Calne through its suburb of Quemerford, along a flat road.

THE WHITE HORSE, CHERHILL.

XXXV

CALNE

Calne (whose name be pleased to pronounce "Carne") is not a pleasing place. Once the seat of a cloth-making industry, it has seen its trade utterly decay, and is only now regaining something of its commerce in the very different staple of bacon-curing. One does not contemn Calne on account of its misfortunes, but it must always have been a slipshod place. "Calne," according to Hartley Coleridge, who described his father's three years' residence there, "is not a very pretty place. The soil is clayey and chalky; the streams far from crystal; the hills bare and shapeless; the trees not venerable; the town itself irregular, which is its only beauty. But there were good, comfortable, unintellectual people in it." With all of which one may agree; save that the "irregularity" of the town is now rather sluttish than beautiful. As for the people, we are but travelling the road, and Calne is only an incident on our way—the people of it something less to ourselves, resembling, in fact, x, an unknown quantity.

The outskirts of Calne are not prepossessing, nor does the long, stony street of mean characterless stone houses that leads to the centre of the little town alter the stranger's view. Calne, in fact, lying so near Bowood, long the seat of the Marquises of Lansdowne, and being their property, wears an abject, servile look. All that makes life worth living is at lordly Bowood; only that which is mean and commonplace is left to Calne. It seems (although one's prejudices are Conservative) as though some vampire were seated near, sucking away the life-blood of the place.

There are two hills just out of Calne; Black Dog Hill, and Derry Hill, and they lead the traveller through picturesque scenery, past one of the lodges of Bowood, and so down into the flat alluvial lands where the Avon flows, and now and again floods out all the dwellers in those levels. The road down there is dreadfully dull to the pedestrian. To the cyclist, on the other hand, who has for these miles past been struggling up hills he cannot climb, and walking down others he dare not coast, the change is one from a penitential pilgrimage to Paradise.

The entrance to the "ancient and royal" borough of Chippenham is hatefully like that into Calne, whose paltry houses are reproduced there. The centre of the town is, however, of a better character, although the streets are cramped and narrow. A singularly foreign air is given to the place by its balustraded stone bridge across the Avon, and if one cares to pursue the Continental tone further it may be found in the huge factory near by, where "Swiss" Condensed Milk, of the "Milkmaid" brand, is manufactured on an immense scale. For the rest, its cheese and corn markets and bacon-curing keep it very much alive, and a modern (and brutally ugly) Town Hall, built in 1856, shows sufficiently well how trade has grown since the time when the picturesque old Town Hall, still standing, was built in the sixteenth century.

THE OLD MARKET HOUSE, CHIPPENHAM.

MAUD HEATH'S CAUSEWAY

The most interesting thing in Chippenham is (to borrow a "bull" for the occasion) outside the town. "Maud Heath's Causeway," a stone-pitched path along the road that runs through the heavy clay lands beside the Wiltshire Avon, extends for four and a half miles, from Chippenham to the summit of Bremhillwick Hill. It was made under the will of Maud Heath, who died about 1474, for the benefit of the market folk resorting to Chippenham, who found the low-lying roads almost impassable in winter. Little is known of this old-time benefactress, but legend supplies the lack of knowledge, and the popular belief is that she was a market-woman who, finding the road from Langley Burrell into the town in so dreadful a state, determined to leave the savings of a lifetime for the provision of a stone causeway, so that future generations might go dry-shod to market.

This causeway goes from the north-east side of the town, and continues through Langley Burrell to Tytherton Kellaways, up the shoulder of Bremhillwick Hill. The portion between Chippenham and Langley Burrell was, for some unexplained reason, not constructed until 1852-3.

According to the inscriptions on the stone posts beside it, the Causeway is held to commence at the Hill, and to end at Chippenham—

> "From this WICK HILL begins the praise
> Of MAUD HEATH'S gift to these highways."

At the other end, next Chippenham, where the road joins those from Malmesbury and Draycott, is another stone, with the inscription—

> "Hither extendeth MAUD HEATH'S gift,
> For where I stand is Chippenham Clift."

Midway, on the bridge over the Avon, is another stone—a pillar twelve feet high, erected by the Trustees in 1698, with the following facts recorded on it:—

"To the memory of the worthy MAUD HEATH, of Langley Burrell, Spinster: who in the year of grace, 1474, for the good of travellers, did in charity bestow in land and houses, about eight pounds a year, for ever, to be laid out on the highway and causeway, leading from Wick Hill to Chippenham Clift."

CHIPPENHAM CLIFT. Injure me not. WICK HILL.

A statue of Maud Heath, a purely imaginary likeness of course, since no portrait of her is known to exist, was set up on a pillar on the summit of Bremhillwick Hill in 1838 by the Marquis of Lansdowne and a local clergyman.

The pillar is forty feet high, and the seated statue on the top of it represents Maud Heath in the costume of the period of Edward the Fourth, with a staff in her hand, and a basket by her side. An inscription bids—

> "Thou who dost pause on this ærial height,
> Where MAUD HEATH'S Pathway winds in shade or light,
> Christian wayfarer in a world of strife,
> Be still—and ponder on the path of life."

The sentiments are admirable, if a little depressing: the verse atrocious.

IMPROVING SENTIMENTS

But worse remains. There are three dials on the pillar, with an inscription on the side facing the rising sun—

> "VOLAT TEMPUS.
> "Oh, early passenger, look up, be wise:
> And think how, night and day, TIME onward FLIES."

Opposite Noon is the advice, "Whilst we have time, do good."

> "QVUM TEMPUS HABEMUS, OPEREMUR BONUM.
> "Life steals away—this hour, O man, is lent thee
> Patient to work the work of Him that sent thee."

For Evening the admonition is not a little alarming—if taken literally.

> "REDIBO. TU NUNQUAM.
> "Haste, traveller! the sun is sinking low;
> He shall return again—but NEVER THOU."

The passing wayfarer might well ask why he should never return along this road!

The late vicar of Bremhill did these metrical paraphrases of the Latin which led so tragically, but whose qualities, as verse, resemble the average of the ordinary Pantomime librettist.

Maud Heath's charity is still in existence, and is now worth about £120 per annum, a sum amply sufficient for keeping her Causeway in repair.

XXXVI

Rowden Hill, a mile out of Chippenham, on the road to Bath, is a welcome drop down into level land again, and would be enjoyable were it not for the bad surface. It is while wheeling such hills and such road-metal that one appreciates at the full the pluck and endurance of those early cyclists who raced across them in the early seventies, making the pace on the high bicycles of those times as gallantly as though the terrible jolting they experienced was really enjoyable. That well-known body of cyclists, the Bath Road Club, has numbered some good sportsmen and rare flyers in its time, and though their pace reads ridiculously slow beside that of these pneumatic-tyred days, the performances of those half-forgotten racers were quite as fine, and, conditions being equal, perhaps finer, than the record rides of recent seasons. There was a time—in August, 1870, to be precise—when two cyclists—Gardner and Fisher, did the double journey of 107 miles each way in five days, and men looked upon them as marvellous riders; so perhaps they were, considering the mechanical limitations of the machines they rode, whose like is not to be seen nowadays save in collections of curios. Equally wonderful were those stalwarts who cut away the hours, piece by piece, until their performances were topped by "Wat" Britten on the "ordinary" in 1880, when he did the double journey in 23 hours. There were those who then thought the last word had been said in the matter of Bath Road Records. They must have been astonished when R. C. Nesbitt's "ordinary" record was made on August 1, 1891, when he covered the out and home course in 15 hrs. 40 mins. 34 secs. Improved methods of manufacture may have had something to do with the smashing character of this new performance; but, even so, consider the extraordinary efforts that must have gone toward getting those figures, which cut Britten's by 7 hrs. 20 mins., and at the same time secured one of the rare victories of the "ordinary" over the "safety" pneumatic-tyred bicycle. For this grand ride defeated Mr. Lowe's, made on a "safety," in 1891 by more than 30 minutes.

CYCLING HISTORY

But that was one of the last expiring efforts of the now obsolete and miscalled "ordinary." It was speedily beaten by J. W. Jarvis, September 20, 1892, who put the figures at 15 hrs. 16 mins. 42 secs.—23 mins. 52 secs. better than the previous best. Then came that hardy Brighton Road record-maker, C. G. Wridgway, whose ride of August 2, 1893, put the clocking at 14 hrs. 22 mins. 57 secs.—a wonderfully heavy lowering of figures. The following year Wridgway established records on both the Brighton and Bath Road within a month; beating his record here of the previous August by his ride on October 4, when he reduced his own time by the astonishing margin of 1 hr. 27 mins. 43 secs.

Time was now cut so close that when W. J. Neasen, of the Anfield Club, essayed the difficult task of lowering it, he only succeeded, on May 11, 1895, in getting inside Wridgway's time by 24 mins. 10 secs., the figures then standing at 12 hrs. 31 mins. 4 secs. H. C. Horswill, of the Essex Wheelers, then beat Neason's performance, in July, 1897, by 24 mins. 34 secs., to be succeeded finally by F. W. Barnes, who on October 30, in the same year, performed the double journey in 11 hrs. 48 mins. 42 secs., and still holds the record.

Among these records of the Bath Road must be mentioned the various essays made by C. A. Smith, of the Bath Road Club, on tricycles. He rode to Bath and back on a three-wheeler, July 16, 1891, in 16 hrs. 13 mins. 18 secs., thus establishing a record, which was beaten four years later—August 23, 1895—by F. Martin, by the narrow margin of 11 mins. 43 secs. These figures in turn were lowered, August 5, 1897, by T. J. Gibbs, Bath Road Club, who accomplished a record of 14 hrs. 18 min.

XXXVII

PICKWICK

And now we come, past the tree-shaded hamlet of Cross Keys, to Pickwick, ninety-seven miles from London, situated at a turning in the road which leads to Corsham Regis, half a mile distant, on the left hand. The traveller, exploring this road for the first time, looks forward with curiosity to seeing a place with so famous a name; but Pickwick, the decayed coaching hamlet, can scarcely be said to "live up to" its literary associations. Strictly speaking, it is not even decayed; but, now that the coaches are no more, flourishes on the "Pickwick Brewery," which makes a brave show down the road. It is an eminently prosperous-looking, stone-built hamlet, a comparatively modern offshoot of the hoary Saxon village of Corsham, which, once on the main road, was thrust into the background when the mail coach came in, and the great highway to Bath was cut on this route, half a mile away.

CROSS KEYS.

It is a curious literary puzzle—How did the title of the "Pickwick Papers" originate? It is a well-ascertained fact that, in 1835, Dickens, then a reporter for the daily press, was sent to Bath to report a speech of Lord John Russell's, that now almost-forgotten statesman being a candidate for representing that city. The future novelist was then but twenty-three years of age, a time of life when impressions of travel are vivid and lasting. Journeying by coach, he had every opportunity for observing places and people; and so it happened that when, a few months later, the now historic publishing firm of Chapman and Hall offered him the literary commission which resulted in the "Posthumous Papers of the Pickwick Club," the story he produced derived many of its features from his own experiences. His recollections had no time to fade, for in March, 1836, the first part of "Pickwick" was published, and others were well on the way. It must ever be a matter of doubt whether Dickens noticed the existence of Pickwick, the place. That he had noted the existence of Moses Pickwick, the coach proprietor of Bath, is obvious enough from the "Pickwick Papers," where Mr. Pickwick and Sam Weller are taking their seats for that City of the Waters.

"'I'm wery much afeerd, sir, that the properiator o' this here coach is a playin' some imperence vith us,' says Sam.

"'How is that, Sam?' said Mr. Pickwick; 'aren't the names down on the way-bill?'

"'The names is not only down on the vay-bill, sir,' replied Sam, 'but they've painted vun on 'em up, on the door o' the coach.'

"'Dear me,' exclaimed Mr. Pickwick, quite staggered by the coincidence, 'what a very extraordinary thing!'

"'Yes, but that ain't all,' said Sam, again directing his master's attention to the coach door; 'not content vith writin' up Pickwick, they puts "Moses" afore it, vich I call addin' insult to injury.'"

There were then, it will be seen, real Pickwicks living in Bath, and the "Moses" Pickwick referred to was an actual person, the great-grandson of one Eleazer Pickwick, who, many years before, had risen by degrees from the humble position of post-boy at the "Old Bear," at Bath, to be landlord of the once famous "White Hart" inn, which stood where the "Grand Pump Room" hotel now towers aloft.

Now comes the long-sought-for connection between place and persons of identical name. Eleazer Pickwick was a foundling. Discovered as an infant on the road at Pickwick, he was named by the guardians, in accordance with an old custom, after the place.

CORSHAM REGIS

Corsham, to which Pickwick belongs, is one of those places which it would be almost an indignity to call a "village," while to name it a "town" would be to give too great an importance to it. It is Corsham "Regis," by virtue of having been a residence of the Saxon Kings; but the Great Western has docked the kingly suffix, and if you were to ask at Paddington for a ticket to Corsham Regis, it is to be feared that the booking-clerk would not recognize the place under its full name.

THE HUNGERFORD ALMSHOUSE, CORSHAM REGIS.

The townlet is a pleasing one, and, always excepting the new and ugly stone villas recently built, it abounds with delightful specimens of domestic architecture of the sixteenth, seventeenth, and mid-eighteenth centuries; fine houses built of Corsham stone in a dignified Renaissance manner, or in the earlier Tudor convention of gables and mullioned windows. Corsham Court, the finest of all, standing in its nobly-wooded park, is Elizabethan, and exhibits the merging of the two periods of Gothic and Renaissance architecture. It was Lady Hungerford, widow of a former owner of Corsham Court, who, in 1672, built the quaint Hungerford Almshouse, close by.

For the rest, Corsham has little history. It was the scene of a mysterious murder in 1594, when a gentleman, one Henry Long, was shot dead, while sitting at dinner amid his friends, by Sir Charles and Sir Henry Danvers, two brothers, who hailed from Dauntsey. The motive was never known, and the assassins were never punished. Six years later, Charles was beheaded for taking part in Essex's rebellion; which seems to be a kind of oblique and fumbling retribution on the part of Providence for his crime. Henry, however, prospered amazingly, and was eventually created Earl Danby, flourishing all his life, as the wicked are, on good authority, supposed to do, "like the green bay tree," and dying in the odour of sanctity, "full of honours, woundes, and daies." He is commemorated in an eloquent epitaph, written by the saintly George Herbert of Bemerton, more than ten years before his (Danvers') death; a circumstance which would seem to prove Herbert a hypocrite and Danvers peculiarly solicitous for his own post-mortem reputation.

Corsham was the birthplace of Sir Richard Blackmore, physician to William the Third, and poetaster, who, says Leigh Hunt, "composed heaps of dull poetry, versified the Psalms, and, by way of extending the lesson of patience, wrote a paraphrase of the Book of Job." What sarcasm!

But Blackmore was read in his day, just as Leigh Hunt was in his, and Fate is sardonic enough (for who at this time reads Hunt's tedious stuff?) to consign critic and criticized to one common limbo of neglect.

XXXVIII

THE BOX TUNNEL

From Corsham the old road used to lead precipitously up to the summit of Box Hill and thence downwards by breakneck gullies, furrowed by rains, and rich in loose stones, into Box. The modern highway goes modestly round the shoulder of the hill. The village of Box has gained an adventitious fame from the celebrated tunnel on the Great Western Railway, which pierces Box Hill, and was, upon its completion, the longest tunnel in England. Compared with later works, it sinks into quite minor importance; but it is still an impressive engineering feat, whether you view it from the railway carriage windows or from the highway. Its length is 3199 yards, or nearly two miles, and the hill rises above it to a height of three hundred feet. Its cost of over £500,000 is no less impressive.

A curious story is told at Box of a platelayer, employed in the tunnel some twenty years ago, who with his gang worked there at night, and slept at Box village in the day. After a while he became engaged to a girl in the village, and the wedding-day was fixed. The vicar of Box, however, was a stickler for red tape, and it appears that he found some technical objection in the fact of the man not sleeping the night in the village. At any rate, he would not perform the ceremony until the Bishop (of Gloucester) compelled him to do so.

ENTRANCE TO BOX QUARRIES.

BOX QUARRIES

At Box we are well within the stone district whose quarries have rendered building-stone from the times of the Roman occupation until the present day. The oolite which comes from here and from the Corsham quarries is a fine grained stone, easily worked, and of a rich cream colour when freshly wrought. As "Bath stone" it is famous, and has made Bath exclusively a city of stone-built houses. In addition, it is sent to all parts of the country, and even exported. The quarries of Corsham and Box are, therefore, the centres of a large and important industry. Box Hill is a mass of this stone, and the tunnel is consequently pierced through it. Three of the quarries are situated in the hill, some of them of great extent. The most extensive is driven into the flank of the hill like a tunnel, and has over three miles of galleries laid with tram-lines: dark, damp places, whose roofs are supported here and there by timber struts. The coldness of these quarry tunnels is remarkably piercing, even in the height of summer.

BOX VILLAGE.

Box seems to have been a favourite country resort of the Romans, away from the crowded streets of *Aquæ Solis*; for on the land that slopes down toward the little Box Brook there have been found many Roman remains, while, only so recently as 1897, the site of a Roman villa was excavated near the south side of the church, with the result of unearthing a complete ground-plan and such interesting relics as mosaic pavements and votive altars.

It is a crowded village to-day, and rather by way of being a town. Lying in a deep hollow, its stone-built houses climb steeply up both sides, with a picturesque glimpse back from where the old village lock-up stands beside the highway to the straggling cottages that line the old road down the side of Box Hill.

Leaving Box we also, in the course of one mile, leave Wiltshire and come into Somerset, with Bath but four miles distant. The Box Brook runs on the right-hand side of the road, the Great Western Railway on the left. Soon, however, the road bends to the right at Bathford, and we come to Batheaston, once a village, but now merely a suburb of Bath, joined to the city by continuous streets.

But there are pretty scenes just off these streets. Bathampton Mill, for instance, just below, on the Avon, with views of the grand circle of hills that enclose Bath.

The picturesquely broken and wooded elevation of Combe Down rises away on the other side of the valley, with Prior Park nestled amid its hanging woods, and the village of Widcombe beneath. At an elevation of five hundred and fifty feet above the sea, it commands views not to be bettered in all the country round. Down below, in the warm steamy atmosphere of the Avon valley, one sees the railway entering Bath on its stone viaducts, and the trains winding in and out along the sharp curves amid the clustered houses. Bathampton lies below there, where the air is languorous and the hillsides hold the heat of the sun. From that sheltered spot the view backwards towards Bathampton Mill and the terraced houses of Batheaston is delightful; the houses that turn their ugly side to the road showing from here, amid their setting of green, like fairy palaces. Lower down the valley the houses cluster more thickly, where the valley widens out into the likeness of a great amphitheatre, and suburbs fade gradually into Bath.

Then, coming to Walcot, the road finally loses all its character as a highway, and tramways, omnibuses, and traffic of every description proclaim the entrance to a populous city.

BATHAMPTON MILL.

XXXIX

BATH

The story of Bath goes back some two thousand years, and has its origin in the myths of ages, in which Bladud figures variously as discoverer and creator of the healing springs. Serious historians are wont to exclude Bladud, and his descent from Brute the Trojan, and Lud Hudibras, the British King, from their pages, for the reason that Geoffrey of Monmouth, the monkish chronicler, who first narrates these stories in his history of Britain, was apt sometimes to confound chronicling with romancing. When, therefore, he tells how Prince Bladud was an adept in magic, and placed a cunning stone in the springs of this valley so that it made the water hot and healed the sick who resorted to them, he is looked upon with a suspicion that is deepened when he goes on to say that Bladud successfully attempted to fly with wings of his own invention from Bath to London, and only came to grief when London was reached, through the strings breaking, so that he fell and was dashed to pieces on the roof of the Temple of Apollo!

Nor is the better known legend of Prince Bladud, the leper, exiled from his father's Court, universally accepted. According to that story, the Prince wandered to where Keynsham now stands, where he became a swineherd, and infected the pigs with his disease. Coming, however, into this valley, the porkers rolled themselves into the hot mud, which then occupied the site of Bath Abbey and the Baths, and were cured. Bladud perceiving this, applied the remedy to himself, with the like result, and returned to his home once more; building a city upon the spot in after years. This happened B.C. 863, and there is a statue of King Bladud, as he afterwards became, erected in the "Pump Room" in 1669; so that any one not subscribing to the truth of this legend had better do so at once, in view of this overwhelming evidence thus afforded.

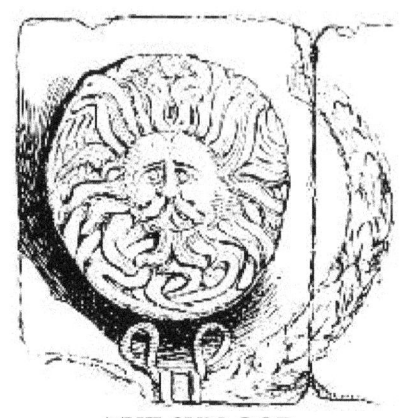

THE SUN GOD.

ROMAN RELICS

We are on more certain ground when we come to the Romans. That great people left too many evidences of their occupation of this island for many doubts to be entertained as to where they settled, or when. Thus, when we assign the close of the first half-century of the Christian era to their discovery of the medicinal properties of these waters, we do so, not from legend, but from the evidence of the buildings they have left behind. It is singular that we do not, as a rule, lay much stress upon the Roman occupation of Britain. Yet it lasted long, and was for nearly four centuries what modern political slang terms "effectual." An advanced civilization reigned here then, and Britain became both a populous and a flourishing colony. The dealings of England with India in the present time form a tolerably close parallel with Rome's conquest of this island, and if we go further and liken the British who remained in the remote places of Cornwall, Devon, and Wales to the fierce Afghans and Chitralis who have troubled us on the borders of Hindostan, we shall by no means strain the similitude. Bath—or rather *Aquæ Solis*, the "Waters of the Sun"[6]—as well as being the one health-resort in Britain for the wealthy Roman colonists who needed such a retreat, was to the Roman officer of that era what Simla and the Hills are to our own military men in India—a place for rest and the restoration of health after the rigours of a hard campaign; with this difference, indeed, that to the Hills they go for coolness, while at Aquæ Solis is the expatriated legionary found both healing springs and a genial warmth after the bleak, inhospitable hills of the Far West or the Farther North.

Discoveries at Bath and in its immediate neighbourhood have proved that there was a sanatorium for invalided officers on Combe Down, and we can well imagine such being conveyed hither, to recover or to die, along the road.

The Baths of the Romans were discovered in 1755, fifteen feet below the surface of the ground; relics of a past magnificence; of a civilization that expired in bloodshed and conflagration. It was in the year 410 that the military forces of Rome left Britain. The weak Romano-British soon retrograded, and, worse than all, the country split up into petty, and mutually hostile, kingdoms. The Baths were neglected, the Arts decayed, and in Britain generally there was not spirit sufficient to withstand the marauding Saxons who finally overwhelmed the country and pillaged and burnt *Aquæ Solis*, just as they had pillaged every other city. It was after the sanguinary Battle of Deorham, A.D. 577, that the three cities of *Glevum* (Gloucester), *Corinium* (Cirencester), and *Aquæ Solis* fell, spoils to the Saxon hosts under Ceawlin. You may search for the site of that great contest at the village now called Dyreham, some fifteen miles north-east of Bath, in Gloucestershire, and from its position it will be at once evident that those three cities must immediately have fallen after that fatal day. That was the cementing of the Saxon power in the West, and a fitting end to a hundred and fifty years of incessant warfare. The British never learned that union means strength; they never had the sense to combine before a common foe, and so the fierce invaders met and defeated them in detail, aided of course by their own fitness for the fight, and by the British incapacity. The Britons were lapped in luxury, and went drunk into battle, so that there was no possible hope for them in fighting the hardy warriors from the North. The wars waged then were wars of extermination, and neither persons nor places were spared. This proud city was levelled with the ground, and the civilization of four hundred years perished by fire in a day. Evidences of that dreadful time were plainly to be seen when the Roman Baths were excavated. They are to be seen even now, at the Museum, together with relics which prove the high degree of civilization that had been attained.

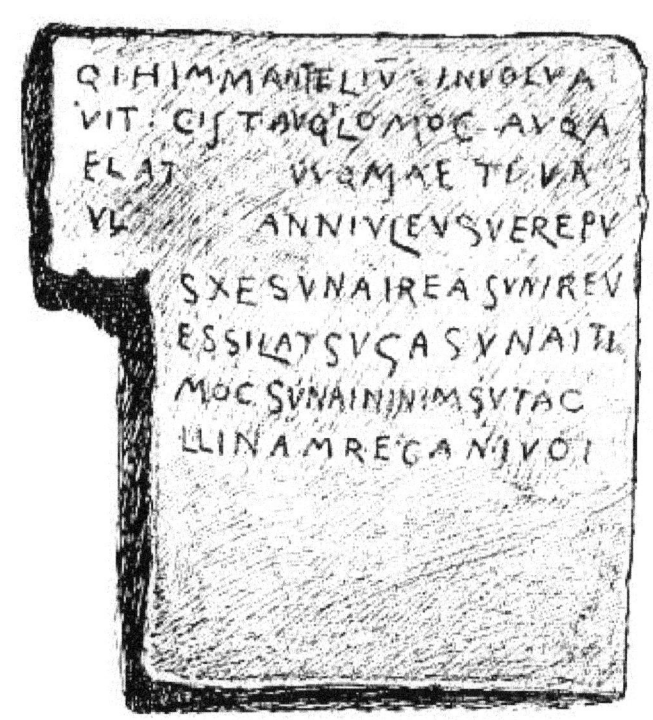

MYSTERIOUS LEADEN TABLET DISCOVERED AT BATH.

Among other marks of progress is an inscribed tablet with an inscription which one authority declares to be the record of a "cure from either taking the waters or bathing, certified by three great men;" while another is equally positive that it is an "imprecation upon nine men, supposed to be guests, who had stolen a tablecloth at the conclusion of a dinner-party." The age of this tablet is fixed "between the second and fifth centuries of the Christian era," which in itself seems to be a wide enough margin. As if, however, this were not already sufficient, there are others, learned in these things, who declare that this relic records how a certain Quintus received 500,000 lbs. of copper coin for washing a lady named "Vilbia"! We are left to take our choice between speculations unfavourable to the personal cleanliness of that lady, or astonishment at the mode and extravagance of the payment. There is, indeed, "another way," as the cookery books have it; but as that involves doubts about the scholarship of professed antiquaries, this third resort may only be hinted at in this place. Who shall decide where antiquaries disagree?

The Saxons were shy of the places they had burnt. Heathens that they were, they generally believed the bloodstained ruins to be haunted by evil spirits, and so built their settlements at some distance away. The site of Bath seems to have been, to some degree, an exception. After lying waste for over a hundred years, it was occupied again, for the fame of its waters had not wholly died out: and "Akemanceaster," as the Saxons called it, entered upon a new lease of life. At that period, too, the Roman Road through Silchester, Speen, and Marlborough acquired its name of Akeman Street; the names meaning, as some would say, the "Sick Man's Town," and the "Sick Man's Road," from "aches" and the fame of the place, even then, as a spot at which to cure them. This has been characterized as absurd, and the derivation more plausibly held to be from a corruption of the Roman word *Aquæ* affixed to the word "maen," or "man," meaning "stone" or "place," and joined to the word "cæster," a form of the Roman "castrum," a fortification; the compound word thus obtained meaning "the Fortified place at the Waters."

ROYAL VISITS

To follow the fortunes of Akemanceaster, or Bath, as it eventually became, through the Saxon period to the present time would be an exercise too prolonged for these pages. That Kings and Princes and ecclesiastics visited it then we know, and that the Normans built a great Abbey church where the present building of Bath Abbey stands is an easily ascertainable fact; but all the comings and goings of the great ones of the earth during the succeeding centuries would form but a bald catalogue. It is only when we come to the middle of the seventeenth century that we need pick up the thread of the narrative again, at the visits of the Queen of Charles the First in 1644; of Charles the Second, the Duke and Duchess of York, and Prince Rupert in 1663; the Queen of James the Second, 1687; and the Princess Anne, 1692; and as Queen Anne, 1702. Truly, a brilliant list for such a small place as Bath then was.

But these Royal visits did not greatly benefit the place, as we may judge when we read that from 1592 to 1692, Bath had increased by only seventeen houses. Why was this? I conceive it to have been owing to the extraordinary apathy of the people of Bath, who had not provided the slightest accommodation for those who then drank the waters. Of what use was it for Sir Alexander Frayser, physician to Charles the Second, sending all his patients hither instead of to Continental health-resorts like Aix, if they had to drink the waters at a pump standing on the open pavement? and imagine the delights of bathing when the Baths were open to the public view, the said public delighting to throw dead cats, offal, and all manner of nastinesses among the bathers!

A local doctor, named Oliver, took up these grievances in 1702, and the Corporation then set about building a Pump Room. This was opened in 1704, and the celebrated Beau Nash having been at about the same period appointed Master of the Ceremonies, the Bath visitors' list showed a decided improvement.

Let us see what the amusements at "the Bath" had been hitherto. The place was devoid of elegant or attractive amusements, and the only promenade for the fashionables who followed Queen Anne to this then outlandish town was a grove of sycamores in which there was a bowling-green, and a band consisting of two performers, playing a fiddle and a hautboy! The courtiers who had deserted St. James's to follow her gouty Majesty to the waters must have cursed their folly when they saw those sycamores and heard that band!

Nash altered all this. He was no King Log, and accordingly soon procured a band of music for the new Pump Room; an Assembly Room for the fashionables to take "tay" or chocolate, to dance, play cards, or to gossip in; and devised a code of manners, if not of morals, for the regulation of his little world, which he ruled with a rod of iron. He regulated everything, from the greatest festivities down to the smallest details of dress and deportment, and not the late M. Worth himself was more autocratic as to what should be worn. It is a familiar story how, the "Dutchess" of Queensbury appearing at a dress ball in an apron (an article of dress which, fashionable elsewhere, he had tabooed), he told her to remove it or leave. The apron was one of point lace, and said to have been worth five hundred guineas; but the Duchess removed it humbly enough, for had not this mighty arbiter of fashions declared aprons "fit only for Abigails" (by which name he meant maidservants to be understood), and who was she that she should dispute such an authority? Then, when the Princess Amelia, daughter of George the Third, begged him to allow another dance after eleven o'clock, what did this potentate reply? Did he humbly grant the request? Not at all; he refused, adding that the laws of Bath were, like those of Lycurgus, unalterable.

XL

BEAU NASH

They say that Nash "made" Bath. That, however, is but partly true. Bath was beginning to make its way when he appeared, and he simply exploited the place. The Moment had come and brought the Man with it, and a tight grip he retained over all fashionable functions for over fifty years. He warred with the high-class rowdies who would have made the place a resort of Mohocks, and elevated "Bath manners" into a school of conduct perfectly well known and imitated, at a distance, in other parts of the Kingdom. They were manners of the most elaborate kind, and if attempted nowadays, it is difficult to conceive how the wheels of the world's business would go round at all. When a meeting took place between a lady and a gentleman, the gentleman inquiring, with a most elaborate bow, after her health, in such terms as "I am vastly honoured to have the pleasure of seeing you; I trust the salubrious airs of the Bath are keeping you in good health;" and the lady replying, "I am much obleeged[7] by your thoughtful inquiries: I protest I am mighty well," it took quite an appreciable time to descend from those rarefied heights of courtesy and come down to the gossip and scandals which were, we are told, among the principal pastimes of this health-resort in the days of powder and patches.

SEVERE MEASURES

But Nash not only saw to it that his fashionable clients behaved themselves. He had to contend with the camp-followers of fashion who swarmed into Bath. Mendicants infested the streets and made the gorge of those delicate eighteenth-century creatures rise with the sight of their rags and diseases. Nash knew that if he did not administer his kingdom severely, and if he allowed many of these stern realities of the world to obtrude upon the sight of the fastidious, the new-found fortunes of Bath would disappear, and his career with them. So, perhaps from an acute sense of the necessity for self-preservation, rather than from any desire to play the autocrat, he imposed his will so thoroughly that he became an unquestioned ruler. He induced the Corporation, which had entrusted him with these powers, to procure an Act in 1739 for the suppression of the beggars. It begins by reciting that "several loose, idle, and disorderly persons daily resort to the City of Bath, and remain wandering and begging about the streets and other places of the said City, and the suburbs thereof, under pretence of their being resident at The Bath for the benefit of the Mineral and Medical Waters, to the great disturbances of his Maj.'s subjects resorting to the said City. Be it enacted that the Constables, petty Constables, Tything-men, and other Peace Officers of the said City ... are hereby empowered and required to seize and apprehend all such persons who shall be so found wandering, begging, or misbehaving themselves, and them to carry before the Mayor, or some Justice, or Justices, of the Peace for the said City; who shall upon the oath of one sufficient witness, or upon his own view, commit the said person or persons so wandering or begging, to the House of Correction for any time not exceeding the space of 12 Kalendar months, and to be kept at hard labour, and receive correction as loose, idle, and disorderlie persons."

THE BATHEASTON VASE.

So there was a reverse to the medal, and a very stringent government prevailed behind the careless, butterfly existence of the age, when literary squibs and lampoons and the gay personalities of Anstey's *New Bath Guide* formed the excitements of the Bath.

A curious relic of this artificial life is to be seen in the Victoria Park in the "Batheaston Vase." This is the name given to a handsome antique placed in a kind of classic temple. The vase was discovered at Tusculum, Cicero's villa, near Frascati, and brought to England during the last century by Sir John and Lady Miller, who then owned a beautiful villa at Batheaston, one of the favourite resorts of the society of that day. Decorated with garlands of bays, the vase was used at Lady Miller's receptions as a depository for verses written by her guests. It was presided over by one of the ladies of the party, posing as the Muse of Poetry, who drew the poetic offerings from its recesses, and, reciting them, crowned the authors of the best effort with bays. The opportunity proved too tempting for some of the wilder spirits, who wrote verses of a ribald and satirical character, better calculated to bring a blush to the cheek of the Poetic Muse than to add to either the morals or the harmony of those gatherings.

XLI

RALPH ALLEN

Among this careless throng there were a few men of will and purpose. Ralph Allen; the two Woods, father and son, architects; and, somewhat later than them, John Palmer, were bold spirits who changed the aspect of Bath and helped to revolutionize the communications of the country.

One of the greatest historical figures of Bath—perhaps even the greatest figure of all—before whom Bladud, Prince of Britain, at one end of the historic period, and Beau Nash at the other, sink into something like insignificance, is that of Ralph Allen. And yet—so arbitrary is fame—that for every ten who could recite you, off-hand, something of the history and achievements of Allen, a hundred could recount the story of Bladud or of Nash. This is not to say that Bath has forgotten her great man. On the contrary, the citizens show you his "Town House" in Lilliput Alley with no little pride, while his great mansion of Prior Park, to the south of the city, and looking down upon it, remains to this day the most princely edifice for miles around. But however mindful Bath may be of him, and although his classic house on the hillside inevitably recalls him to the memory of Bath people, the fact remains that Allen's is a name comparatively unknown to Bath's visitors.

That he deserves a record in these pages must be conceded, for he it was who first established a regular postal service between one provincial town and another, and carried letters along the cross-roads, which, until his time, had been utterly neglected by the Post-office.

It is a singular thing that to Bath should have belonged both Ralph Allen and John Palmer; the men who respectively developed the postal service and founded mail-coaches. It is true that Allen was not a native of Bath. His father was an innkeeper at St. Blazey, in Cornwall, and in that far western county he first learned the routine of a post-office, in the early years of last century. He was eleven years of age when he was placed with his grandmother, the post-mistress of St. Columb, and his industry in keeping the accounts secured him the good word of the district surveyor, who procured the lad an appointment as assistant to the post-master at Bath. Fortune favoured him, and when the post-master died, Allen was appointed in his stead. He had not long become post-master before he matured a scheme for developing the "bye" and cross-road posts, which should bring profit to himself and convenience the community. He proposed to "farm" these posts and pay the Government an annual sum for the privilege, leaving the direct posts between London and the provinces in the hands of the Post-office. A "bye" post was one between provincial towns; a cross-road post was one that lay off the half-dozen post routes then existing.

It was in 1719 that Allen, then but twenty-six years of age, made his proposal to the Government. The postage on those descriptions of letters had hitherto amounted to £400 per annum. He was prepared to give £6000 yearly, and to work the posts for a period of seven years, in consideration of receiving the whole of the revenue during that term. His offer was accepted, and the contract took effect from June 21, 1720. How Allen procured the funds for his enterprise is not known, but he must have had substantial financial support, since his first quarter's expenditure in establishing his system amounted to no less a sum than £1500, while the salaries of the staff he got together totalled a further £3000 per annum.

Allen was a man of a modest and retiring habit, but with the greatest confidence in himself. He needed all his confidence, and all the untiring industry and vigilance that were his, for when three years of the seven had expired he found himself a loser by a small amount, and when the contract lapsed, his gain was quite inappreciable. Yet he renewed it for another seven years, convinced that the better facilities he had provided for the carriage of letters must needs lead to great developments. He was right: the correspondence of the country grew, and in 1741 we find him bidding £17,500 per annum for another term of seven years. He continued thus until his death in 1764, in receipt, for many years, of an income of not less than £12,000 a year on his post-office enterprise alone.

POSTAL SERVICES

Those were the times of the real post-boys. All letters were carried by mounted messengers, since the stage-coaches then running (where they existed at all!) were not fast enough, frequent enough, or sufficiently safe for the purpose. A side-light is thrown upon the average "speed" of these stage-coaches, not then considered speedy enough, by the onerous condition in Allen's contract that the mails were to be carried by his post-boys "at not less than five miles an hour."

Allen was in the forefront of Bath enterprise, and was associated with John Wood, the elder of the two architects of that name, in rebuilding the city. Before their time it had been a place of mean streets and winding alleys, the out-at-elbows remains of Gothic times. As a result of their labours, and the labours of their immediate successors, Bath renewed her youth in a revived Classicism. Among the monuments of that time, Prior Park is conspicuous. It was built by John Wood in 1743 for Allen, whose great object in erecting this veritable palace was to demonstrate the qualities of the building-stone on his Combe Down property. Here he entertained some of the foremost literary men of his time: Pope, Fielding, Warburton; and is enshrined by Fielding as "Squire Allworthy" in "Tom Jones," and by Pope in the lines—

> "Let low-born Allen, with ingenuous shame,
> Do good by stealth, and blush to find it fame."

The situation, and the front elevation of Prior Park, form together, perhaps, the noblest grouping of classic architecture and romantic scenery to be found in England. It was a time tinged with romanticism of an artificial kind which generally showed itself in affected and objectionable ways. But this artificiality was a matter of deportment merely. Literature was practised then, and Architecture flourished in the land.

PRIOR PARK.

"SHAM CASTLE"

There is another work of Allen's crowning the hill at Bathwick, which serves to show at once the romantic and the artificial signs of the times. Allen looked out from the windows of his Town House upon the bare hilltop, and thought how the view would have been improved had there been a ruined castle showing against the sky-line. Accordingly he built such an one, and there it is to-day; and if you don't know it to be a ruin built to order, it is very impressive indeed—at a distance. If, however, you know it to be a Sham

Castle (which, by the way, is the name of it), romance immediately flies, abashed. There it stands, on its wind-swept heights, naked and unashamed; a frontage with nothing behind it; an empty mask, with crossbow slits from which arrows never were discharged, and battlements scarce more substantial than the pasteboard turrets that furnish the stage in romantic drama. If hypocrisy be indeed the homage that Vice pays to Virtue; then, by parallel reasoning, here is homage of the most flattering kind paid to Gothicism by an age that above all things prided itself on the way it fulfilled its classic ideals. It was a common failing of the time; and possibly, if attention had been called to it, a ready answer might have been found in the retort that "consistency is the bugbear of little minds."

"SHAM CASTLE."

XLII

But to return to the Beau, who seems to represent Bath more fully than any other person connected with its history. In his old age Nash fell upon evil times. Ruined by his own folly and extravagance, he had no opportunities of retrieving the position, for he had lived to see the friends of his more fortunate era pass away, and to witness the arrival of a younger generation which regarded his laws with indifference, if not with open contempt. His last years were eked out with the aid of a pittance of £10 a month given him by the Corporation of the city for which he had done so much, and a new Master of the Ceremonies presently reigned in his stead.

In his declining days, Bath had altogether changed from the place it had been when in the zenith of his power. It had, for one thing, grown out of all knowledge, architecturally. The Grand Circus, parades, terraces, squares, all manner of finely designed houses, had sprung up. Smollett, in "Humphrey Clinker," makes Squire Bramble peevishly recount those changes, and say, "The same artist who planned the Circus has likewise projected a crescent: when that is finished, we shall probably have a star; and those who are living thirty years hence may perhaps see all the signs of the zodiac exhibited in architecture at Bath."

BATH SOCIETY

Then the select society of fifty years before had given place to a very mixed concourse, if we are to believe the same authority: "Every upstart of fortune, harnessed in the trappings of the mode, presents himself at Bath, as in the very focus of observation. Clerks and factors from the East Indies, loaded with the spoil of plundered provinces; planters, negro-drivers, and hucksters, from our American plantations, enriched they know not how; agents, commissaries, and contractors, who have fattened, in two successive wars, on the blood of the nation; usurers, brokers, and jobbers of every kind; men of low birth, and no breeding, have found themselves suddenly translated into a state of affluence, unknown to former ages; and no wonder that their brains should be intoxicated with pride, vanity, and presumption. Knowing no other criterion of greatness but the ostentation of wealth, they discharge their affluence, without taste or conduct, through every channel of the most absurd extravagance; and all of them hurry to Bath, because here, without any further qualification, they can mingle with the princes and nobles of the land. Even the wives and daughters of low tradesmen, who, like shovel-nosed sharks, prey on the blubber of those uncouth whales of fortune, are infected with the same rage of displaying their importance; and the slightest indisposition serves them for a pretext to insist on being conveyed to Bath, where they may hobble country-dances and cotillons among lordlings, squires, counsellors, and clergy. These delicate creatures from Bedfordbury, Butcher-row, Crutched-friars, and Botolph-lane, cannot breathe in the gross air of the lower town, or conform to the vulgar rules of a common lodging-house: the husband, therefore, must provide an entire house or elegant apartments in the new buildings. Such is the composition of what is called fashionable company at Bath."

XLIII

What, however, of the literary celebrities, visitors or residents, or of the statesmen, the naval and military commanders, who were frequenting Bath at the time when that jaundiced criticism was penned. Dr. Johnson was then taking the waters, which are said by a later authority to taste of "warm smoothin'-irons;" Gainsborough alternately painted and bathed; while the Earl of Chatham and his still greater son; Nelson, Wolfe, Sheridan, and Goldsmith, Wordsworth, Southey, Jane Austin, and Landor, helped to sustain the repute of this, which Landor called the next most beautiful place in the world to Florence, well on into the next century.

THE BATH OF LONG AGO

A diarist of over a century ago tells us how he went to Bath, and what he saw and did there. This was the Reverend Thomas Campbell, a lively Irishman (notwithstanding his Scottish name), who journeyed to England in 1775, and visited Johnson and other literary bigwigs in London, coming to Bath on April 28, to take the waters. The coach set out from the New Church in the Strand (by which, no doubt, Saint Mary-le-Strand is indicated) at six o'clock in the morning, and came to Speenhamland ("Spinomland," says the clergyman in his diary), where they lay. The country, he remarks, was very rich from London to this place, yet it was so level that there was scarce a good prospect the whole way, unless Clieveden, near Maidenhead Bridge could be so called.

OLD PULTENEY BRIDGE.

When the coach resumed its journey the next day—the passengers, doubtless, lightened in pocket by that "long bill" of the "Pelican" at Speenhamland—the bleakness of Marlborough Downs communicated itself to the air, and from Newbury to Cottenham,[8] a distance of nearly thirty miles, the countryside was very bare of trees and herbage, in addition to being the worst land this Irishman had seen in England, and certainly swarming with beggars. For miles together the coach was pursued by them, from two to nine at a time, almost all of them children. They were more importunate than those of Ireland, or *even* those in Wales. Poor Taffy!

When our traveller reached Bath he rejoiced greatly, and, the next day being Sunday, went to the Abbey Church with other fashionables, and heard a sorry discourse, wretchedly delivered. Afterwards, in the Pump Room, where the yawning visitors were assembled, he met Lady Molyneux, who asked him to dinner, where he spent the pleasantest day since he came to England, for there were five or six lively Irish girls who sang and danced, and did everything but agree among themselves. "Women," remarks our diarist, "are certainly more envious than men, or at least they discover it upon more trifling occasions, and they cannot bear with patience that one of their party should obtain a preference of attention; this was thoroughly exemplified this day. One of these, who was a pretty little coquet, went home after dinner to dress for the Rooms, and her colour was certainly altered on returning for tea; they all fell into a titter, and one of them (who was herself painted, as I conceived) cried out, 'Heavens, look at her cheeks!'" This, truly, was unkind, and more certainly indiscreet. The young lady with the startling cheeks subsequently sang a song, which somewhat surprised the clergyman, from its breadth of idea, but the other ladies, and matrons too, "were kicking with laughter." Presently they all went home, the ladies most affectionate toward one another, and, says Mr. Campbell, "it is amazing what pleasure women find in kissing each other, for they do smack amazingly."

A TORY PROPHECY

The worthy clergyman seems to have been introduced to the less dignified circles of fashion. The general tone of the more exclusive sets was by no means so lively, for it was about this time that the Indian nabobs, the Civil servants, the retired officers of the Army and Navy and the East India Company began to discover Bath and to settle there, filling the place with Toryism and grumblings about "the services going to the dogs, sir." Here is a Tory prophecy, not yet verified: "There is one comfort I cannot have at Bath," said the Duke of Northumberland in 1779. "I like to read the newspapers at breakfast, and at Bath the post does not come in till one o'clock; that is a drawback to my pleasure." "So," said Lord Mansfield, "your grace likes the *comfort* of reading the newspapers—the *comfort* of reading the newspapers! Mark my words. A little sooner or later those newspapers will most assuredly write the Dukes of Northumberland out of their titles and possessions, and the country out of its king. Mark my words, for this will happen."

As a prophecy, it may readily be conceded that this is an extremely bad shot, and that Lord Mansfield by no means, either figuratively or literally, inherited the mantle of Elijah. A hundred and twenty years have passed since then, and there are still dukes who have not been reduced to sweep crossings or keep chandlers' shops. True, if they have not come down so far in the world, it is in some cases owing to American dollars; but that is not the doing of the newspapers, one way or the other. As I have just remarked, that was a Tory prophecy, and though my Toryism is, I trust, of the most mediæval and crusted kind, and wholly beyond cavil, it may frankly be admitted here that the Party never has shone in prophecy. Nor, for that matter, has any party. The only seers are the leader-writers, and they never see beyond their noses.

So Principalities and Powers and Titles are at least as powerful as ever they were, and—cynical fact—certain newspaper proprietors have been raised to the House of Peers; a thing, we may be sure, that Lord Mansfield never contemplated.

Many other things, however, have happened in the meanwhile. Agitation does not pay so well as it did. The newspapers which were to do such dreadful things have greatly increased in number, if not in power, and the contents of them have changed radically; other times, other manners, as a glance at even the advertisements of that date will prove.

XLIV

OLD ADVERTISEMENTS

The advertisement columns of a paper just over a century old often afford amusement to those who come upon them. The manners and customs of those times and these are so different that the very quaintness of our forefathers' attitude of mind brings a smile upon our faces, although those eighteenth-century forbears of ours were really very serious people indeed, and took life, for the most part, like a dose of medicine, while we are apt to go to the other extreme and take it like champagne. No doubt our great-great-grandfathers would think the most sedate of us not a little wild could they witness how we live to-day, while, in our turn, we look back upon their times, and think times and people alike brutal. We wonder what sort of people they were who could, in this England of ours, offer a "Black boy for sale—docile and obedient. Answers to the name of Peter." Yet such advertisements were common on the front page of our newspapers once upon a time. Slavery was then a matter of course, and to have a black page for her very own was my lady's hall-mark of "quality." Sometimes such advertisements were embellished with little figures supposed to represent nigger-boys.

The race of African negroes has either improved in good looks since then, or else the engravers of that day were not very careful in portraiture. But, indeed, black pages were almost as common as pet dogs, and were advertised in very much the same way, and these blocks were not portraits at all, but just printers' stock illustrations. The printer of a hundred years ago kept a curious little assortment of advertisement blocks. If a ship was about to sail for the colonies, it was advertised for weeks beforehand, and in a corner of the announcement was placed something that purported to be an illustration of the vessel. It generally looked like a Spanish galleon strayed from the Armada of two hundred years previously, and passengers would have been quite justified in not booking berths on so antiquated an affair.

But perhaps the most amusing advertisements are the "Run away from his Home" and the "Stolen" varieties, also adorned with illustrations. It speaks very little for the morality of that age when we say that the ordinary newspaper printer also kept these blocks in stock.

And, indeed, they seem to have frequently been required. Here is one example out of many in the newspapers of that age:—

"STOLEN
Out of the Stable of ROBERT COLGATE,
The 24th instant August, 1780

A black horse, rising five years old, thirteen Hands and a Half High, Star in his forehead, small Ears, Mane stands up rough, being lately rubbed off, long Tail, hangs his Tongue out often on the Road, good Carriage; also a good Saddle, marked Barnard, with Spring Stumps.

"Whoever gives Information, so that the Said Horse may be had again, shall receive TWO GUINEAS REWARD."

It would scarcely be possible to identify the stolen horse from the accompanying cut. He has no long tail, as described in the advertisement, and his tongue *doesn't* hang out. Moreover, he is burdened with a quite imaginary thief, who has a property devil whipping him on. The "awful example" hanging from the gibbet appears to be made of bolsters, and to have had, not a drop too much, but scarcely enough.

The party with hands bigger than his head, who is here seen striking a dramatic attitude, is not a Howling Swell, although he wears his hair parted in the middle. Appearances here (as usually was the case in the old advertisements) are deceptive, and so far from being a Swell, Howling or otherwise, he is really a Heartless Villain, for he is one of two labourers who have—

"RUN AWAY.

And left their families chargeable to the Parish of CLAVERTON,

THOMAS GARNER, Labourer, about five feet seven or eight Inches high; wears his own Hair, of a light Brown Complexion; hath lately, or is now belonging to the Militia.

"And EDWARD BROWNING, Labourer, about five Feet four or five Inches high, wears his own Hair, of a dark complexion; was one of Lord North's Soldiers in the last War.

"Whoever will apprehend either, or both of them, and conduct them to the Parish Officers of Claverton aforesaid, shall receive HALF A GUINEA for each or either of them, and THREEPENCE per Mile for every Mile they shall travel with them."

History does not relate whether or no these gay deceivers were ever captured. If those who sought them relied upon the illustration, it would seem quite likely that they never were!

XLV

THE ABBEY

The Abbey is the very centre of Bath. Round it cluster the Municipal Offices, the Baths, and the Pump Room, and along the broad pavements invalids are drawn in Bath chairs—one of the five articles with which the name of the City is indissolubly linked. When Bath chairs, Bath chaps, Bath stone, and Bath buns are no longer so distinguished, then will come the final crash. One need not insist so greatly upon Bath Olivers, because they are not in every one's mouth, either literally or figuratively; although, to be sure, they are much more exclusively a local product than "Bath" buns; while "Bath" bricks are not made at Bath, but at Bridgewater.

The surroundings of Bath Abbey are strikingly Continental in appearance, for that great church stands in a flagged *place*, instead of being set in a green and shady close, as usually is the case in England. Its surroundings have always been thronged, from the time when the Flying Machines crawled, to when the last of the mail coaches drew up in front of the "White Lion," in the Market Place hard by, or at the "White Hart," which stood until 1866, where the "Grand Pump Room" Hotel now rises. The story of the Abbey is too long for these pages; but it is remarkable at once for being one of the very latest Gothic buildings in the country; for its possessing windows so large and so many that it has been called the "Lantern of England;" for its central tower, which is not square, being eleven feet narrower on its north and south sides than those to the east and west; and for the prodigious number of small marble and stone memorial tablets on its interior walls—tablets so many that they gave rise to the famous epigram by Quin:—

> "These walls, so full of monument and bust,
> Shew how Bath waters serve to lay the dust."

BATH ABBEY: THE WEST FRONT.

Quite distinguished dust it is, too. Noblemen and dames of high degree; Admirals of the Blue, the White, the Red; legal, and military, and clerical dignitaries, and all manner of Civil servants, mostly of the mid-eighteenth century, and chiefly hailing from India and the Colonies, as described with much pomp and circumstance on their cenotaphs which so thickly cover the walls, and spoil the architectural effect. "The Bath," was the solace of their kind, returning from the Tropics with nutmeg livers, gout, and autocratic ways. At "the Bath" they resided on half-pay, drank the waters, supported the local doctors, quarrelled with their neighbours, and consistently damned all "new-fangled notions," until death laid them by the heels.

There must have been—if we are capable of believing their epitaphs—some paragons of all the virtues in those times, and Bath seems to have claimed them all. Here, for instance, is Alicia, Countess of Erroll, "in whom was combined every virtue that could adorn human nature." She died young; the world is too wicked for such.

"JACOB'S LADDER"

Bath Abbey is remarkable in one respect far above all the minsters and cathedrals of England. As you stand facing the great West Front, which looks so grim and grey upon the stony courtyard that stretches before it, you see, flanking the immense west window, two heavy piers, terminating in turrets. On these piers are carved the singular representations of "Jacob's Ladder" that have given the Abbey a fame even beyond the merit of its architecture. From near the ground-level, almost to the turrets, this curious carving stretches, battered long years ago by the fury of an age which prided itself on its enmity to "superstitious images," and reduced by the further neglect of more than two hundred years to an almost shapeless mass. The origin of this curious decoration is found in the vision of Bishop Oliver King, who restored the then ruined Abbey in 1499. In this vision, by which he was induced to undertake the great work, he saw angels ascending and descending a ladder, and heard a voice say, "Let an Olive establish a Crown, and let a King restore the Church." He interpreted this as a Divine injunction to himself to repair the Abbey, and accordingly commenced the work; dying, however, before it was completed. The "ladders" have sculptured angels on them, while on the wall above the arch of the great window is represented a great concourse of adoring angels, with a figure of God in glory in their midst. Many of the figures have their heads knocked off; but the whole of this sculpture is shortly to be restored.

XLVI

Bath entered upon a dead period about 1820. For a long while the newer and more easily reached glories of Brighton had taken the mere fashionables away, and even the waters were less favoured. Continental wars had ceased, and unpatriotic Britons flocked to foreign spas instead; Bath looking idly on and letting its customers go.

THE ROMAN BATH, RESTORED.

It was some ten years later that Dickens visited Bath. From what he saw there he drew his portraits of place and persons in the "Pickwick Papers;" and the impression after reading them is undoubtedly one of faded gentility.

So it remained until after the visit of the British Association in 1864, when the advice of the scientific men to the Corporation—to bring back business by providing more up-to-date accommodation—was laid to heart, and improvements begun. Since then the City has steadily climbed back again to the favour of invalids and the medical profession, and new Baths and all manner of modern appliances, a new railway station, and an air of an enlightened modernity, bid fair to keep Bath successful against all foreign competition for a long time to come.

MODERN BATH

Since this Renaissance of thirty-five years ago was begun, many things have happened at Bath. Roman remains, more extensive than ever the bygone generations suspected, have been discovered, and excavations have lain bare baths long covered up by shabby and altogether undistinguished buildings. Judicious restoration has preserved the great Roman Bath, long a scene of wreck and shattered stones, and has brought it into use again. This restored Bath affords perhaps the most picturesque view in the City, for from its margin one may gaze upwards and see to great advantage the beautiful tower of the Abbey soaring aloft; its late Gothic architecture contrasting piquantly with the classic elegance of that restored bathing-place, while the reflections of the columns deep down in the quiet pool give a singularly complete sense of restfulness.

All this modern prosperity is, no doubt, very gratifying, but prosperity means much building, and Bath has now its suburbs; uncharted stretches of new villas, isolated, or in streets, that climb the hillsides of Combe Down, Beechen Cliff, and Lansdowne, and help to destroy Macaulay's well-known, if something too overdrawn, architectural picture of Bath, as "that beautiful City which charms even eyes familiar with the masterpieces of Bramante and Palladio, and which" (horrible literary solecism!) "the genius of Anstey and of Smollett, of Frances Burney and of Jane Austen, has made classic ground."

Bath, indeed, was a jewel set in midst of her picturesque amphitheatre of rocky and wooded hills; but now that those hills and those woods are being covered with houses whose architecture is less calculated to "charm the eyes familiar with the masterpieces of Bramante and Palladio" than were the buildings of a century and a half ago, the setting of the jewel is by way of becoming tarnished. Now, also, it has been reserved to these times of cheap railway carriage of goods for brick houses to be seen at Bath; the one place in the world where brick never had an opportunity until these latter days of the "combine" of the allied "Bath Stone Firms," which has raised the price of Bath stone, so that in certain cases it has been found cheaper to bring bricks from the Midlands to build houses in Bath than to use the stone quarried on the spot. So, in the wilderness of new suburbs, the traveller who is whisked away by rail to Bristol may see, to his astonishment, amid the stone houses, rows of the most undeniable red-brick villas. And thus has come the spirit of what the late Professor Freeman was pleased to call "modernity" over Bath, once the peculiar preserve of stone and Classicism.

Footnotes

[1] Stranger still, the chief informer was named Porter.

[2] Tawell had poisoned his sweetheart, who, before dying, had time to denounce him to her friends. They pursued him to the station, but when they arrived there the train had gone. The telegram sent was in these words:—

"A murder has just been committed at Salt Hill, and the suspected murderer was seen to take a first-class ticket for London by the train which left Slough at 7.42 p.m. He is in the garb of a Quaker, with a brown great-coat on, which reaches nearly to his feet. He is in the last compartment of the second-class carriage."

At Paddington he took a City omnibus, but the conductor was a policeman in disguise, and dogged his footsteps from one coffee-house to another, which he is supposed to have entered for the purpose of setting up an *alibi*. At length, as he was stepping into a lodging-house in the City, the police tapped him on the shoulder, with the question, "Haven't you just come from Slough?" Tawell confusedly denied the fact, but he was arrested, with the result already recounted.

[3] Lord Iveagh's name is Guinness. Unfortunately for the thoroughness of the jest, there are but thirteen chapters in the Epistle to the Hebrews.

[4] It was about 1630 that the town of Marlborough obtained a new grant of arms in place of its old shield of a "Castle *argent*, on a field *sable*." The new shield, still in use, is heraldically described as—"Per Saltire, gules and azure. In chief, a Bull passant, argent, armed or. In fess, two Capons, argent. In base, three greyhounds courant in pale, argent. On a chief, or, a pale charged with a Tower triple-towered, or, between two Roses, gules. Crest—On a wreath, a Mount, vert, culminated by a Tower triple-towered, argent. Supporters: two Greyhounds, argent." These arms are intended to perpetuate the memory of the ancient custom in Marlborough of the aldermen and burgesses presenting the mayor for the time being with a leash of white greyhounds, a white bull, and two white capons.

[5] "There are many pleasanter places, even in this dreary world, than Marlborough Downs when it blows hard; and if you throw in beside a gloomy winter's evening, a miry and sloppy road, and a pelting fall of heavy rain, and try the effect, by way of experiment, in your own proper person, you will experience the full force of this observation."

The traveller's horse stopped before "a road-side inn on the right-hand side of the way, about half a quarter of a mile from the end of the Downs.... It was a strange old place, built of a kind of shingle, inlaid, as it were, with crossbeams, with gabled-topped windows projecting completely over the pathway, and a low door with a dark porch and a couple of steep steps leading down into the house, instead of the modern fashion of half a dozen shallow ones leading up to it."

[6] That the Romans knew the city we call Bath as *Aquæ Solis*—the "Waters of the Sun"—we learn from the ancient history of Britain. A highly interesting light upon this is furnished by the sculptured stone discovered some years since, and now in the local museum, which shows a decorative representation of the head of the Sun God from whose face radiate sun-rays, alternately with serpents.

[7] Once the recognized pronunciation of the word. The great Duke of Wellington was probably the last who spoke it thus.

[8] He meant Chippenham.

Milton Keynes UK
Ingram Content Group UK Ltd.
UKHW040859050124
435493UK00006B/925